CW00943046

WELCOME TO

BASKETBALL LEGENDS:
THE NEXT GENERATION

Lunar Press is an independent publishing company that cares greatly about the accuracy of its content.

If you notice any inaccuracies or have anything that you would like to discuss, then please email us at lunarpresspublishers@gmail.com.

Enjoy!

© Copyright 2024 - All rights reserved.
The content contained within this book may not be reproduced, duplicated or transmitted without direct written permission from the author or the publisher.

Under no circumstances will any blame or legal responsibility be held against the publisher, or author, for any damages, reparation, or monetary loss due to the information contained within this book, either directly or indirectly.

Legal Notice:
This book is copyright protected. It is only for personal use. You cannot amend, distribute, sell, use, quote or paraphrase any part, or the content within this book, without the consent of the author or publisher.

Disclaimer Notice:
Please note the information contained within this document is for educational and entertainment purposes only. All effort has been executed to present accurate, up to date, reliable, complete information. No warranties of any kind are declared or implied. Readers acknowledge that the author is not engaged in the rendering of legal, financial, medical or professional advice. The content within this book has been derived from various sources. Please consult a licensed professional before attempting any techniques outlined in this book.

By reading this document, the reader agrees that under no circumstances is the author responsible for any losses, direct or indirect, that are incurred as a result of the use of the information contained within this document, including, but not limited to, errors, omissions, or inaccuracies.

COMPLETE THE SET

IF YOU ENJOY THIS BOOK, DIVE DEEPER INTO THE

BASKETBALL LEGENDS UNIVERSE WITH

BASKETBALL LEGENDS & BASKETBALL'S GREATEST

STORIES!

'For a man that has won so many championships, scored an endless number of points, and is often called the GOAT, Michael Jordan didn't have many better games than that one. He has since admitted that it was the hardest thing he ever had to do on a basketball court, and that's saying something!'

Basketball's Greatest Stories

CONTENTS

TIP OFF...

Deciding on the hottest prospects in any sport is hard, but when it comes to basketball, it's even harder! Why? Because stats and numbers can only tell us so much. Some players don't truly blossom until they are 26 or 27, and sometimes older! Still, basketball is one of the biggest sports in the world, so there will always be a massive pool of young players to choose from!

This book aims to pick the 20 most promising young prospects in the world. It wasn't easy, but that's the amazing thing about sports—we get to decide for ourselves.

Of course, hundreds of young players didn't make the cut. There are rookies who might end up being amazing one day but haven't quite yet reached their full potential, but the 20 men and women in this book are all exceptional—that's the one thing everyone can be sure of!

Also, some players come along once in a while with the potential to be the greatest of all time, the GOAT, the best of the best, but things happen that stop their progress, such as injuries or personal issues. Some of those on this list have already struggled with injury, such as Zion Williamson, and as fans, we can only hope that they find full fitness later in their careers and we get to see how amazing they can be!

Magic Johnson, Kobe Bryant, and Stephen Curry never won Rookie of the Year, so it's safe to say that sometimes players take a little longer to become true superstars. For others, it took a trade to another team later in their career before everything clicked. For some, it's a new coach or teammate that helps them make that one last change to their game that makes them go from "Hmm, maybe" to "Oh, wow, that player's the best I've ever seen!"

Then there are players like LeBron James and Michael Jordan who come along young, and it simply can't be denied that they'll be great. When they grew to become the Hall of Famers we know today, it was a beautiful thing to see. Watching a world-class NBA or WNBA player in their prime is a wonderful thing; it can be poetry in motion. There is every chance that several of the players on this list will be spoken about in the same way in years to come.

You will see as you start to read the biographies in the following pages that none of the players are numbered. That's because it's pretty much impossible to separate them. However, nothing is stopping you from deciding who goes where. That's the fun part!

Maybe you think Jaren Jackson Jr. is the most outstanding prospect in basketball, or perhaps it's Ezi Magbegor. Chet Holmgren has burst onto the NBA scene, while Rhyne Howard is already seen as one of the faces of the WNBA. Victor Wembanyama nearly won gold with France at the 2024 Paris Olympics, almost single-handedly carrying the team. And Paolo Banchero, the guy who was three feet tall as a toddler, is an Orlando Magic icon despite still being so young!

It's never easy to choose on lists like this, but with 20 of the best prospects in basketball all in one place, it might be a little easier!

So, sit back, learn, and most of all, enjoy yourself. Basketball is one of the most entertaining sports on the planet, and so are the stories of the players who make it so great!

TYRESE
MAXEY

CAREER

**PHILADELPHIA
76ERS**
2020-PRESENT

NBA DRAFT
2020
1ST ROUND
21ST OVERALL PICK

TROPHY CABINET

NBA ALL-STAR	X1
NBA MOST IMPROVED PLAYER	X1
NBA SPORTSMANSHIP AWARD	X1
SECOND-TEAM ALL-SEC	X1
SEC ALL-FRESHMAN TEAM	X1
MCDONALD'S ALL-AMERICAN	X1

BIOGRAPHY

BORN	NOV 4, 2000
NATIONALITY	AMERICAN
BIRTHPLACE	DALLAS, TEXAS
HEIGHT	6 FT 2 IN (1.88 M)
POSITION(S)	PG / SG

At six foot three and over 200 pounds, Tyrese Maxey is surprisingly quick and nimble*. His muscular shoulders and arms allow him to take heavy contact and remain standing, while his ability to rapidly turn defense into offense has made him one of the most dangerous prospects in the NBA.

Born in Dallas, Texas, on November 4, 2000, Tyrese was the only boy of four kids. His father played college ball for the Washington State Cougars, so Tyrese grew up surrounded by basketball. His idol was Dwyane Wade, and when Tyrese's father saw how much his son wanted to style his play on Wade's, he set up a training schedule to help him as much as possible.

By sixth grade, Tyrese had already started to shine. He won an Amateur Athletic Union (AAU) Championship game despite breaking his pinky finger a few days before the big game. Even though his doctor strapped it up and told him he shouldn't play, Tyrese knew he couldn't miss the Final and played anyway, using his other hand to dribble and shoot!

Tyrese started out as a shooting guard, starring for South Garland High School for several years. In his sophomore year, he averaged 22.5 points, 5.5 rebounds, 3.6 assists, and 2.5 steals per game. He improved even more the following year, averaging 22.5 points, seven rebounds, 3.1 assists, and 4.5 steals.

His performances that second year saw South Garland reach the Texas state tournament for the first time. Tyrese was excellent in the semifinal. Sadly, his 46 points weren't enough to stop South Garland from losing.

It wasn't just on the court where Tyrese shone. He was a brilliant student who finished at the top of his class. He knew that getting a good education was very important, and he wanted his mind as sharp as his basketball skills.

After achieving his dream of becoming a McDonald's All-American, Tyrese began to choose his college. Despite being so good in high school, he wasn't as recruited as some of the other young players in America that year. He was ranked 14th in the country. In the end, he decided on the University of Kentucky.

Tyrese made his college debut at Madison Square Garden in a Champions Classic win over the Michigan State Spartans. It was an insane venue for a kid to play his first game, and to make it even more special, it fell on Tyrese's 19th birthday. He came off the bench to score an incredible 26 points, a record for a freshman debut.

Kentucky was the perfect fit for Tyrese, and in his debut season, the Wildcats won the regular season championship. This meant that they would be the number one seed, and they were most people's pick to win it. Sadly, the Wildcats never got to finish the tournament, as the COVID-19 pandemic shut the world down.

Tyrese declared for the 2020 NBA Draft and was selected 21st overall by the Philadelphia 76ers. After an impressive preseason, head coach Doc Rivers admitted Tyrese was too good for the developmental program and that he would be one of the team's main bench guys for the upcoming season.

Three weeks after signing his rookie contract, Tyrese made his NBA debut in the opening game of the regular season. He played 11 minutes against the Washington Wizards, recording six points, two rebounds, and two assists.

With COVID-19 still keeping the world on lockdown and many players sick or injured, the 76ers found themselves in trouble for the January 9 game against the Denver Nuggets. League rules state that a team must have at least eight players to officially play a game; otherwise, they forfeit. The 76ers managed to scrape together eight players—just!

It all meant that Tyrese had earned his first start, and he grabbed the opportunity with both hands! He was superb, putting up 39 points in 44 minutes as the 76ers won 115–103. It was the most points scored by a rookie in their first start since 1970!

As the season came to an end, most of the injured and sick players had returned, so Tyrese found himself on the bench again. He played a few minutes here and there as the 76ers reached the Eastern Conference Semifinals, only to lose a seven-game epic to the Atlanta Hawks.

Tyrese spent the summer of 2021 in the NBA Summer

League. He wanted to play as much ball as possible to keep improving. His aim was to be a starter by the time his second regular season rolled around! It worked, and with Tyrese as a shooting guard, the 76ers reached the 2022 playoffs once more.

The first game against the Toronto Raptors was Tyrese's breakout moment. He put up 38 points in a 131–111 victory, setting another record. The 76ers won the series, with Tyrese averaging 21.3 points per game. He was also making a name for himself as a brilliant three-point scorer.

The Miami Heat put an end to the 76ers' dreams in the semis, but Tyrese still finished as the team's leading scorer. He was definitely a starter now!

Tyrese continued to improve through the following season. His 44 points in a 112–90 win over the Raptors that October made him just the third player in 76ers history to score at least 40 points in a game before the age of 23. He topped this in the 2022–23 season, putting up 50 points against the Indiana Pacers.

On February 1, 2024, Tyrese was named to his first All-Star Game. That same day, he scored 51 points in a 127–124 win over the Utah Jazz. He finished the 2023–24 season with the NBA Most Improved Player Award and the NBA Sportsmanship Award, finally getting the recognition he deserves.

As you will see, all of the players in this book have bright futures, and Tyrese is no different. Unlike many of the others, Tyrese wasn't ranked number one during high school, but he proved that rookie rankings are just someone else's opinion. Hard work and dedication will always win out! Tyrese Maxey is proof of that.

ALIYAH BOSTON

CAREER

INDIANA FEVER
2023-PRESENT

WNBA DRAFT
2023
1ST ROUND
1ST OVERALL PICK

TROPHY CABINET

WNBA ROOKIE OF THE YEAR	X1
WNBA ALL-STAR	X2
WNBA ALL-ROOKIE TEAM	X1
NCAA CHAMPION	X1
NCAA TOURNAMENT MOP	X1
AP PLAYER OF THE YEAR	X1
HONDA SPORTS AWARD	X1

BIOGRAPHY

BORN	DEC 11, 2001
NATIONALITY	AMERICAN
BIRTHPLACE	U.S. VIRGIN ISLANDS
HEIGHT	6 FT 5 IN (1.96 M)
POSITION(S)	PF / C

Aliyah Boston is the type of player who could play in any position and make it seem natural—she's just that good. Even though she is still basically a rookie, she has proven herself to be one of the best in the WNBA already. The Indiana Fever's forward has won so many individual honors and awards that a separate book would be needed to fit them all in! Let's just say that she is on this list because she is one of the hottest prospects in basketball!

Aliyah was born on December 11, 2001, in Saint Thomas, U.S. Virgin Islands. Her childhood was pretty unsteady, and she spent much of it moving between her aunt's home in New England and her mother's house in Saint Thomas. When she was 12, she moved to New England permanently with her older sister, Alexis. After that, the two girls didn't see their parents as much.

Alexis was also an outstanding basketball player, and when Aliyah was 9, she watched Alexis play a game on the street with her friends. After that, Aliyah was hooked. She played every minute she could, and soon, she was the best in her neighborhood, often playing with boys and girls who were a lot older than her.

When Aliyah started at Worcester Academy, a high school, she really took off. Before then, she had only played for fun. Now, she was playing organized basketball for the first time, and the structure and better players around her really suited her style. By the end of 2017, she had won the Massachusetts Gatorade Player of the Year award. She won it again in 2018 and 2019, winning the New England Preparatory School Athletic Council Class A Championship in 2019 too.

That 2019 season was special. In addition to winning the championship and being named the player of the year for the third year running, she was also named consensus All-American. To top it off, she played in the McDonald's All-American Game and the Jordan Brand Classic*.

By the time she finished high school, Aliyah was a five-star recruit and ranked third in the ESPN HoopGurlz 2019 class. She committed to the South Carolina Gamecocks, where she would have a fantastic college career.

In her first game at the University of South Carolina, on November 5, 2019, she posted the first triple-double by a freshman in the history of the National Collegiate Athletic Association (NCAA). Now, that's one way to make a name for yourself! Then, in the 2019 Paradise Jam*, she won the Reef Division MVP after putting up 20 points and 13 rebounds as the team won the championship.

Aliyah finished her 2019 by winning gold with the USA at the International Basketball Federation (more commonly called FIBA, short for Fédération Internationale de Basketball) Under-19s Basketball World Cup!

On January 20, 2020, she recorded her eighth double-double of the season, then followed this up with two more in the next couple of weeks. She was named Freshman of the Year as she led the Gamecocks to their first-ever number one season. She then began her sophomore year in the same way, hitting several more double-doubles in the opening games. Her game improved each week, and she became one of the most dominant players in her position.

Aliyah got tired of double-doubles, so she decided to hit the program's first triple-double in Southeastern Conference (SEC) play! Seriously, though, her 16 points, 11 rebounds, and 10 blocks in a win over Georgia were spectacular. After this, she returned to double-doubles, recording three in a row to bring her season total to 10!

She was insane in the Gamecocks' SEC Basketball Tournament Championship win. She recorded 15 points and 11 rebounds in the Semifinals against Tennessee before putting up 27 points and 10 rebounds in the Finals against Georgia. She finished as SEC Tournament MVP, recording double-doubles in all three games.

Throughout college, Aliyah also studied for a career in communications*, finishing with a degree. She hopes to have a career in broadcasting when she stops playing, and she got good practice when she joined the NBC Sports studio to cover the Big Ten and Notre Dame women's basketball games during her rookie season.

After two more years of college dominance, Aliyah

declared for the 2023 WNBA Draft. She was selected first overall by the Indiana Fever, and it took her just four games to announce herself as one of the most dangerous players in the league! Aliyah won the WNBA Rookie of the Month the first time of asking and then did it again the following month. She was now a true WNBA star, and she was still just a rookie!

A great rookie season saw Aliyah named to her first WNBA All-Star Game, and even though she won the Rookie of the Month award one more time, she couldn't help the Fever reach the playoffs. Still, the team was getting better each week, which was mostly down to Aliyah.

Even with the team not reaching the playoffs, she was still unanimously named WNBA Rookie of the Year, which is a pretty amazing thing to do for a player on a team that didn't do too well. She also became the first rookie in WNBA history to lead the league in field goal percentage with 57.8%!

Aliyah was just 22 at the time of this book being written, so her journey is only beginning. With so many individual awards already sitting proudly on her shelves and several gold medals with the USA at many different levels, the sky really is the limit for Aliyah Boston. It's safe to say that one day, she will be considered a legend of the WNBA!

LUKA DONCIC

CAREER

REAL
MADRID
2015–2018
↓
DALLAS
MAVERICKS
2018–PRESENT

NBA DRAFT

2018
1ST ROUND
3RD OVERALL PICK

TROPHY CABINET

NBA ALL–STAR	X5
ALL–NBA FIRST TEAM	X5
NBA ROOKIE OF THE YEAR	X1
NBA SCORING CHAMPION	X1
NBA ALL–ROOKIE FIRST TEAM	X1
ALL–FIBA WORLD CUP TEAM	X1
EUROLEAGUE CHAMPION	X1

BIOGRAPHY

BORN	FEB 28, 1999
NATIONALITY	SLOVENIAN
BIRTHPLACE	LJUBLJANA
HEIGHT	6 FT 7 IN (2.01 M)
POSITION(S)	PG / SG

At 25, Luka Dončić is a little older than most of the people on this list, but it would be impossible to leave him off it. You see, some of the European players have a little longer to wait until they reach the NBA, as they usually come over later in their career, so they are still NBA rookies.

Luka Dončić is six foot seven and 230 pounds, yet he moves on the court like a much smaller guy. He's amazing in pick-and-roll play, and his court vision is unreal. He can shoot, pass, and defend, and he is devastating in the offense too.

Born on February 28, 1999, in Ljubljana, Slovenia, Luka adored basketball. His father played professionally for several European teams and was also a coach. According to his parents, Luka first held a ball when he was 7 months old and was throwing it through a small hoop by the time he was 1!

It wasn't just basketball that he loved, though. Luka was great at several sports, including soccer, which he had to quit when he got too tall. All it meant was that now he had time to put all of his practice into basketball! He started playing organized basketball at 7, usually with kids who were 10, which never seemed to bother him.

Growing up, his heroes were Greek legend Vassilis

Spanoulis and LeBron James. He loved the way they played, and his dream was to be as good as them one day.

When he was 8, his father signed with local team Union Olimpija. The team's second coach asked Luka to practice with the youth program and then moved him up three levels to the Under-12 team after seeing him play for just 16 minutes! Luka even practiced with the Under-14 team from time to time, even though they were nearly twice his age!

At just 13, Luka was signed by Real Madrid, one of the biggest franchises in Europe. He chose the #7 jersey in honor of his idol, Vassilis Spanoulis. He quickly rose through the youth ranks, winning the Minicopa Endesa* and the youth championship. He averaged 24.5 points, 13 rebounds, four assists, and six steals per game. After one season, he was moved to the Under-18 team despite only turning 14!

If that wasn't insane enough, Luka soon made his pro debut. On April 30, 2015, having just turned 16 two months before, Luka played his first game for Real Madrid! By the following season, he was a starter. The season after that, he won the Euroleague and was also named MVP!

Luka left Madrid in 2018 and declared for the NBA Draft. The Atlanta Hawks selected him third overall before instantly trading him to the Dallas Mavericks for the trading rights to Trae Young. A lot was expected of Luka, but he has always been ice cold under pressure.

Luka made his debut not long after signing rookie terms. Playing in the NBA had been his lifelong dream. He recorded 10 points, eight assists, and four rebounds in a 121–100 loss to the Phoenix Suns. Three days later, he put up 26 points and six rebounds in a 140–136 win over the Minnesota Timberwolves, becoming the youngest 20-point scorer in Mavericks' history.

On December 28, he became the first rookie to make seven three-pointers in a single game. His performances during this period led to him being named Western Conference Rookie of the Month. He followed this up with his first triple-double, recording 18 points, 11 rebounds, and 10 assists.

At the end of his rookie season, Luka had finished fourth in triple-doubles, joint with his idol LeBron James! He was unanimously selected for the All-Rookie First Team and named Rookie of the Year. His first year in the NBA really couldn't have gone any better for him!

As Luka continued to improve, so did the Mavericks. The triple-doubles kept coming, and then on December 8, 2019, Luka broke Michael Jordan's record of consecutive games with at least 20 points, five rebounds, and five assists when he reached 19 in a row!

The records continued after that. In his first-ever playoff game, he put up 42 points against the LA Clippers, which was the most for a postseason debutant. He also added 17 rebounds and 13 assists to his impressive points tally. If that wasn't enough, he hit a buzzer-beater three-pointer to seal a 135–133 win in the same game! It pretty much made him a Mavericks legend already.

The 2020–21 season saw the Mavericks win the division title as Luka's numbers continued to rise. He reached 5,000 points at just 22 and continued his form into the playoffs, breaking triple-double records. Still, the Mavericks were shocked by the Clippers in the first round and crashed out.

On August 10, 2021, Luka signed the largest rookie extension contract in history, giving him a little over $200 million! He celebrated two days later by recording his 44th career triple-double!

Luka reached his first Western Conference Finals at the end of the season, and despite leading the team in points, rebounds, and assists 10 times during the playoffs, he couldn't help the Mavericks overcome the Golden State Warriors. He was selected to his third consecutive All-NBA First Team, becoming just the third player since the merger to do so.

Sadly, the Mavericks didn't even make the playoffs in the 2022–23 season, but Luka continued to dominate on his own. He was selected for his fourth consecutive All-NBA First Team, but it would have meant little to him, seeing as the team didn't do well.

The Mavericks were back in the playoffs the following season, and they reached the NBA Finals, only to lose heavily to the Boston Celtics.

Luka Dončić is now one of the best players in the NBA. He is the Mavericks' not-so-secret-weapon! Does he deserve his place on this list? Of course he does! He is already a legend on the Mavericks, and pretty soon, he could even be an NBA Hall of Famer.

EZI
MAGBEGOR

CAREER

CANBERRA CAPITALS
2017–2018
↓
MELBOURNE BOOMERS
2018–2020
↓
SEATTLE STORM
2020–PRESENT
↓
SOPRON BASKET
2022–2023
↓
USK PRAGUE
2023–PRESENT

TROPHY CABINET

WNBA CHAMPION	X1
WNBA ALL–STAR	X1
ALL–WNBL FIRST TEAM	X1
WNBA ALL–DEFENSIVE SECOND TEAM	X2

WNBA DRAFT
2019
1ST ROUND
12TH OVERALL PICK

BIOGRAPHY

BORN	AUG 13, 1999
NATIONALITY	AUSTRALIAN
BIRTHPLACE	WELLINGTON, NEW ZEALAND
HEIGHT	6 FT 4 IN (1.93 M)
POSITION(S)	F / C

At six foot four, Ezi Magbegor has always had the size to be dominant in the WNBA. But when you add in her ability to read the game as it unfolds and her shot-blocking, Seattle Storm's lockdown defender and center is already one of the best players in the league. Her performances with Australia at the Paris Olympics in 2024 helped the team win bronze, and if she continues to improve the way she has, she could one day be remembered as one of the greats.

Born in Wellington, New Zealand, on August 13, 1999, to Nigerian parents, Ezi had a childhood filled with many different cultures. Her family moved to Australia when she was 6, where Ezi soon discovered basketball. She played any chance she could get, and by the time she was a teenager, there was lots of talk around the local courts about the tall girl who could shoot and defend with ease.

At school, Ezi was the best player on the girls' team by a mile, so she asked to play with the boys instead. She did for a while, but pretty soon, the boys were demanding that she be moved back to the girls' team because she was just too good for them!

Ezi was six feet tall by the time she turned 15, which sadly led to bullying and teasing. It didn't help when she grew another four inches the following year. Ezi never backed down, though. She stayed proud, and she surely knew that deep down, the kids who picked on her were just jealous of her talents on the court.

Near the end of high school, she earned a place on Basketball Australia's developmental team. They practiced at the Centre of Excellence, where only the hottest prospects in Australia play. While in the South East Australian Basketball League (SEABL), Ezi started to get noticed for her defensive talents and her leadership skills. She's always been a born winner, which comes out whenever she steps onto the court.

While at the Centre of Excellence, Ezi got her first taste of international basketball. She starred for the Australian team at the 2015 FIBA Under-19 World Championship in Russia. Most players were 18 or 19, but Ezi still shone despite having just turned 16.

Soon after, she helped the team win the 2015 Oceania Championship in Spain, averaging 18 points per game. Australia beat the USA in the Final, which was even more special because the Americans were on a 27-game winning streak! Ezi's performances brought her to the attention of all the WNBA franchises and colleges.

The Canberra Capitals, an Australian franchise, signed her at the end of her time in the SEABL, and she quickly became their most important player. She stayed there for one season (2017) before signing for the more professional Melbourne Boomers on a three-year contract. Several of the best colleges in America tried to get her, but she wanted to make sure she was ready before she took the huge step of moving to the States.

Ezi had a busy 2017. After her big move to the Melbourne Boomers, she played her first game for Australia's senior team. Her ability to break up play was essential as Australia played several buildup games as they prepared for the 2018 Commonwealth Games*. The hard work paid off, and Australia took home the gold, beating their fierce rivals England in the Final.

The following year, Ezi won the first of her three Betty Watson Australian Youth Player of the Year awards. If WNBA scouts hadn't been watching her before, they certainly were now!

After a few years with the Boomers, Ezi finally felt like she was ready for the WNBA. She signed for the Seattle Storm in 2020, quickly slotting into an already brilliant team. With Ezi's dominant style, the Storm were hard to beat. After smashing the Minnesota Lynx 3–0 in the Western Conference Finals, they did the same in the WNBA Finals, winning the championship with a 3–0 victory over the Las Vegas Aces.

That championship win was extra special for Ezi, as the final game of the series fell on her 21st birthday!

The high of winning the championship in her rookie season became a low that summer when Australia struggled at the 2020 Olympics in China. They barely got out of their group before losing to Team USA in the Quarterfinals. Ezi returned for the 2021 WNBA season more determined than ever!

Throughout her short WNBA career, Ezi has also split her time between other leagues, signing with Hungarian team Sopron Basket in 2022. In her single season with Sopron, she won the championship, gaining huge experience in the WNBA offseason. The following year, she signed up for the Czech team USK Praha, where she would play during the WNBA break.

After just two years of playing in the WNBA, Ezi was named the Betty Watson Australian Youth Player of the Year for the second time, scoring 38 of the 42 votes!

Her second season with the Storm was another success, as the team won the Commissioner's Cup in 2021. Her dream of becoming a WNBA All-Star would still have to wait despite many fans believing she was ready. But Ezi has always been a hard worker, and when she sets her mind to something, she usually achieves it. She might not have made the All-Star Game, but she was named All-Defensive Second Team in 2022 and All-WNBA First Team. She also won her third Betty Wilson Australian Youth Player of the Year award!

By 2023, Ezi couldn't be ignored anymore. She was leading a new-look Storm team, and most people saw her as the leading player. She was named to the WNBA All-Star Game at the end of the season, completing an incredible journey through many countries and leagues. But that journey is still only just beginning. Ezi is basically a rookie, so who knows how many All-Star Games she'll star in?

After more success with the Storm, Ezi helped Australia to bronze at the 2024 Paris Olympics. It was yet another medal for her already-bulging trophy cabinet!

JA
MORANT

CAREER

MEMPHIS GRIZZLIES
2019-PRESENT

NBA DRAFT

2019
1ST ROUND
2ND OVERALL PICK

TROPHY CABINET

NBA ALL-STAR	**X2**
ALL-NBA SECOND TEAM	**X1**
NBA MOST IMPROVED PLAYER	**X1**
NBA ROOKIE OF THE YEAR	**X1**
NBA ALL-ROOKIE FIRST TEAM	**X1**
CONSENSUS FIRST TEAM ALL-AMERICAN	**X1**

BIOGRAPHY

BORN	AUG 10, 1999
NATIONALITY	AMERICAN
BIRTHPLACE	DALZELL, SOUTH CAROLINA
HEIGHT	6 FT 2 IN (1.88 M)
POSITION(S)	PG

Much like Luka Dončić, Ja Morant has been on the scene for a while, so it's hard to remember that he's still a young man. The Memphis Grizzlies' point guard is quick, agile, and explosive. His ability to cut through defenses makes him so dangerous, and his acrobatic point-scoring has made him a fan favorite.

Temetrius Jamel Morant was born on August 10, 1999, in Dalzell, South Carolina. Both of his parents were superb basketball players themselves. His mother, Jamie, was a point guard in high school, and his father, Tee, played semi-pro after college. Tee was close to going pro in Europe, but Jamie fell pregnant with Ja, so Tee gave up his dream to focus on raising his family.

Ja earned his nickname as a child when his parents shortened his middle name, and from that point on, he was simply known as "Ja"! During his childhood, Ja played basketball every chance he got, often practicing in the backyard with his father for hours on end. Tee taught him how to perfect his step-back jump shots, which can still be seen in his game today.

Ja attended Crestwood High School in Sumter, South Carolina. Although he was the best player in his school, finishing his time as Crestwood's all-time leading scorer, he wasn't even ranked in the class of 2017 by ESPN, 247 Sports, or Rivals. In fact, only one Division I college offered him a scholarship.

In the end, Ja chose Murray State. His debut came against Brescia University in a 118–61 win. A month later, he recorded his first college career double-double, then followed this up two weeks later with a triple-double.

By his sophomore year, Ja was starting to finally get the recognition he deserved. Several NBA scouts watched him as he broke Murray State's record for triple-doubles. But it wasn't just his scoring that was being noticed. Ja was and is a very unselfish player, and he knows there is no "I" in "team." By the end of the season, he led the NCAA Division I in assists.

After helping Murray State to the 2019 tournament, Ja decided to end his college career with a couple of years to spare and enter the NBA Draft. Murray State retired his jersey soon after.

Ja was selected second overall in the 2019 NBA Draft by the Memphis Grizzlies. He signed a four-year $39.6 million contract and made his debut on October 23, 2019—a 120–101 loss to the Miami Heat. Ja played well, recording 14 points, four rebounds, and four assists. He also managed a steal and a block.

It took him just a few weeks to put up his first triple-double as he helped the Grizzlies beat the Washington Wizards 106–99. He continued his form throughout the season, leading the league in assists and being named Rookie of the Year!

Ja's second season was even more impressive, and the team started to improve right alongside him. On December 23, 2020, he put up 44 points, adding nine assists, two rebounds, and two steals to his fine performance. The team lost to the San Antonio Spurs, but Ja was quickly becoming the Grizzlies' most important player.

The Grizzlies reached the playoffs for the first time in four years after a dramatic overtime win against the Golden State Warriors. In that game, Ja recorded 35 points, six rebounds, and six assists. Two days later, he played his first-ever playoff game, putting up 26 points, four rebounds, and four assists in a 112–109 upset in Game 1 against the Utah Jazz.

Despite Ja being even better in Game 2 (he scored 47 points), the Grizzlies lost the series in five games.

Ja caught fire in the 2021–22 season. In under two weeks, he had 37-point, 40-point, and 41-point games. In the last of these, he scored six three-pointers as the Grizzlies got revenge on the Los Angeles Lakers with a 104–99 victory. By the end of the regular season, he had won the NBA Most Improved Player Award.

The Grizzlies reached the playoffs again, with Ja playing brilliantly as he put up the franchise's first postseason triple-double in Game 3 against the Timberwolves. In Game 5, he scored the game-winning layup with just one second remaining, ending the game with 30 points, 18 of which were scored in the final quarter!

Ja couldn't help the Grizzlies overcome the Golden State Warriors in the second round, as a knee injury in Game 3 ended his season. Soon after, he signed a new $200-million-plus five-year deal.

The Grizzlies were soon playoff regulars, but they couldn't make that last step to the Finals. In the 2022–23 season, the Lakers beat them in six games. Ja continued to add to his huge triple-double collection, but the Finals continued to be just out of reach.

As for the 2023–24 season, Ja would probably like to forget it. Suspensions and injuries basically ruined it. After returning from suspension in December, Ja then injured his shoulder less than a month later, with the surgery keeping him out for the rest of the season. It was frustrating for him, but he will surely come back stronger than ever!

Ja Morant is proof that scoring points isn't everything. The players who build up the play from defense are just as important. Ja enjoys an assist as much as a dunk, and that makes him the perfect team player. Without team players, there is no team!

CHET
HOLMGREN

CAREER

OKLAHOMA CITY THUNDER
2022–PRESENT

NBA DRAFT

2022
1ST ROUND
2ND OVERALL PICK

TROPHY CABINET

NBA ALL-ROOKIE FIRST TEAM	**X1**
CONSENSUS SECOND TEAM ALL-AMERICAN	**X1**
WCC DEFENSIVE PLAYER OF THE YEAR	**X1**
WCC NEWCOMER OF THE YEAR	**X1**
FIRST-TEAM ALL-WCC	**X1**

BORN	MAY 1, 2002
NATIONALITY	AMERICAN
BIRTHPLACE	MINNEAPOLIS, MINNESOTA
HEIGHT	7 FT 1 IN (2.16 M)
POSITION(S)	C / PF

He might be known as a center or power forward, but there is so much more to Chet Holmgren's game than that. Despite his huge size, Chet moves, shoots, jumps, and handles like a guard. At seven foot one, his blocking and rebounding, mixed with his three-point shooting, have made him one of the hottest prospects in the NBA.

Chet Holmgren was born in Minneapolis, Minnesota, on May 1, 2002. His father, who was seven feet tall, was a superb player who starred for the University of Minnesota. When Chet was old enough to walk, his father helped him with his training, and he continued to be his biggest influence throughout his childhood.

Chet attended Minnehaha Academy, where he quickly became one of the school's best players. He was six foot two by the sixth grade, and by the ninth grade, he was six foot nine. One of Chet's teammates at Minnehaha was Jalen Suggs, and together, they formed a devastating partnership.

By his sophomore year, Chet was averaging 18.6 points and 11 rebounds per game. During a televised game against Sierra Canyon High School, Chet recorded nine points, 10 rebounds, and 12 blocks. Sierra Canyon was a nationally ranked team with players like Bronny James, Ziaire Williams, and Brandon Boston Jr., so the standard was insane. Minnehaha's win against such talent brought Chet to the attention of many colleges and NBA scouts.

After Jalen Suggs committed to Gonzaga, Chet did the same. His college career caught fire right away, as he recorded 14 points, 13 rebounds, seven blocks, and six assists in a 97–63 victory over Dixie State. Those were the highest numbers from a college debutant in 25 years!

There were rumors that he would enroll in the University of Minnesota like his father, Dave, who had played 57 games for the Golden Gophers. In the end, his choice of Gonzaga proved the right one. It was the perfect match!

His international career was also instantly successful. He represented the USA at the FIBA Under-19 Basketball World Cup, averaging 11.9 points, 6.1 rebounds, 3.3 assists, and 2.7 blocks per game. The USA won gold, and Chet earned MVP honors.

Chet stayed in college until the end of his freshman year, when he declared for the 2022 NBA Draft. Having already hit seven foot one and with college numbers through the roof, Chet felt like he was ready to turn pro. He was right!

The Oklahoma City Thunder selected Chet as the second overall pick. He quickly joined the team's 2022 NBA Summer League roster, putting up 23 points, seven rebounds, four assists, and six blocks in a 98–77 win against the Utah Jazz. He broke the record for most blocks in a single Summer League game on his debut.

He signed a rookie-scale contract on July 5, 2022, but sadly suffered an injury a month later. It was so bad that he would miss the whole regular season. Suffering such a devastating setback so early in his career could have destroyed him, but Chet has always been determined to beat the odds.

Nearly a year and a half after signing his rookie contract, Chet finally made his NBA debut on October 25, 2023. He put up 11 points and four rebounds in a 124–104 win over the Chicago Bulls. Two days later, he recorded 16 points, 13 rebounds, and seven blocks in a 108–105 victory against the Cleveland Cavaliers. It was the most blocks in a single NBA game by a rookie.

A month after his debut, Chet was named NBA Rookie of the Month! His performances had the Thunder's fans excited, and he was soon being tipped as a future franchise legend. Despite being so tall, his grace on the court has always made him a joy to watch. But it's his passion for winning that really sets him apart!

Chet's first full season was fantastic. He played all 82 regular season games as the Thunder reached the playoffs. They swept the New Orleans Pelicans in the first round, which made them the youngest team to ever qualify for the Semifinals. It was also the franchise's first playoff series win in nearly a decade.

The Thunder were then shocked by the Dallas Mavericks in the Semifinals, losing in six games. Chet played all ten games in the playoffs, cementing himself as one of Oklahoma's star players. If his rookie season had been a total bust because of injury, his second was a dream.

Chet Holmgren has all the talent to one day make him an NBA legend. If he can stay injury-free, that's almost a certainty!

ANTHONY
EDWARDS

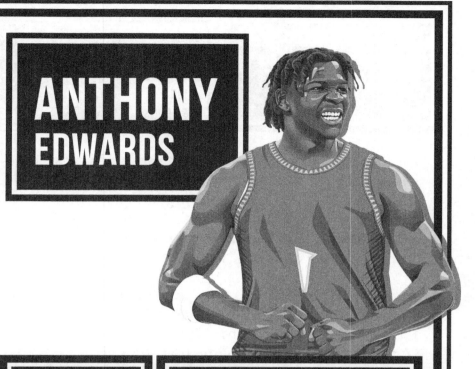

CAREER

**MINNESOTA
TIMBERWOLVES**
2020–PRESENT

NBA DRAFT

2020
1ST ROUND
1ST OVERALL PICK

TROPHY CABINET

NBA ALL-STAR	X2
ALL-NBA SECOND TEAM	X1
NBA ALL-ROOKIE FIRST TEAM	X1
SECOND-TEAM ALL-SEC	X1
SEC ROOKIE OF THE YEAR	X1
MCDONALD'S ALL-AMERICAN	X1

BIOGRAPHY

BORN	AUG 5, 2001
NATIONALITY	AMERICAN
BIRTHPLACE	ATLANTA, GEORGIA
HEIGHT	6 FT 4 IN (1.93 M)
POSITION(S)	SG

Although a shooting guard, Anthony Edwards could easily excel in many other positions. He can lead the break like any of the best point guards and mix things up when transitioning to a small forward. He is already a two-time NBA All-Star, making him a Minnesota Timberwolves superstar.

Anthony Edwards was born on August 5, 2001, in Oakland City, Atlanta, Georgia. When he was 3, his father began calling him "Ant," which then became "Ant-Man." It was a nickname that stuck!

Football was actually Anthony's first love, and he was a brilliant quarterback. He was also an excellent running back and cornerback. Anthony played youth football for the Atlanta Vikings, where he became one of the hottest prospects in the country. But basketball was quickly becoming his passion, and in his teens, Anthony made the switch.

By the time he hit high school, Anthony was obsessed with basketball. He played every moment he could. Although he first attended Therrell High School, he soon moved to Holy Spirit Preparatory School, as he felt they had a better academic* program. He knew that education was vital for anyone who wanted to be the best version of themselves. In his first year at Holy Spirit, the team won the championship.

While he was in the eighth grade, Ant's mother and grandmother both died in a short space of time. The pain nearly broke him, as it would anyone. Anthony was raised by his sister and brother, who helped him get through it. In the end, he turned the negative into a positive and used the pain to make him stronger.

Anthony was rated a five-star recruit and the best shooting guard in the 2019 class. After heavy recruiting, he decided to play for the Georgia Bulldogs. One of the main reasons he chose Georgia was because they were coached by Tom Crean, who had trained two of Anthony's favorite players, Dwyane Wade and Victor Oladipo. Anthony's dream is to one day be as good as his heroes.

He made his Bulldogs debut on November 5, 2019, putting up 24 points, nine rebounds, and four steals in a 91–72 victory over Western California. It was an insane debut and the most points scored by a debutant since Hall of Famer Dominique Wilkins in 1979. By the final game of his rookie season, Anthony led the team in points, rebounds, and steals.

Anthony decided to finish his college career after his freshman year and declare for the 2020 NBA Draft. Sadly, the Draft was delayed by five months due to the COVID-19 pandemic, so he had to wait until he found out who would sign him. When the Draft finally happened in November, the Minnesota Timberwolves selected him as the number one overall pick.

A month later, he made his NBA debut, putting up 15 points, four rebounds, and four assists in 25 minutes as the Timberwolves beat the Detroit Pistons 111–101. By

March, he was flying, hitting a career-high 42 points in a game against the Phoenix Suns. It made him the third-youngest player in NBA history to score 40-plus points in a game. He ended his rookie season by finishing second in the Rookie of the Year voting behind LaMelo Ball, who we will cover next!

The 2021–22 season saw the Timberwolves improving alongside their new star. In November, he put up seven three-pointers while scoring 48 points in a 123–110 loss to the Golden State Warriors. He followed it up later in the season with a 49-point game against the Spurs. The Timberwolves reached the playoffs but lost 4–2 to the Memphis Grizzlies.

The Timberwolves reached the playoffs again in the 2022–23 season, where Ant put up 41 points in a 122–113 loss to the Denver Nuggets in Game 2 of the first round. His 41 points were a franchise playoff record. When he recorded 36 points in the next game, he joined Kobe Bryant with the second-most playoff points before the age of 22!

The Timberwolves couldn't get past the Nuggets, who went on to win the NBA Championship, but Ant finished the season with All-Star honors.

Ant changed his jersey from #1 to #5 before the 2023–24 season, and his form continued to improve. He started the season like a man possessed, being named NBA Western Conference Player of the Week in November as he led the team to a 4–0 run of wins. On February 1, he was named to his second All-Star Game, and a couple of months later, he put up a career-high 51 points in a 130–121 win over the Washington

Wizards.

The Timberwolves reached the playoffs yet again, this time facing the Phoenix Suns. In Game 4, Ant scored 31 of his 40 points in the second half, and the Timberwolves won their first playoff series in 20 years! They then faced the Nuggets in the Semifinals, the team that had beaten them the previous year. Ant was fantastic, scoring 43 points in Game 1 and 44 in Game 4, as the Timberwolves won a classic series 4–3 to reach only their second-ever Conference Final!

Sadly, the Finals were a step too far, and the Timberwolves lost to the Dallas Mavericks 4–1. The loss hurt, but Ant and the Timberwolves have been improving each year. Who would bet against them reaching the NBA Finals next year?

After the disappointment of the 2023–24 Playoff Finals loss, Ant traveled to France for the 2024 Olympics, where he helped the USA to gold. In a career that is only a few years old, Anthony Edwards has already become an Olympic champion and a two-time NBA All-Star! The future is definitely bright for Ant-Man!

LAMELO BALL

CAREER

PRIENAI
2018
↓
LOS ANGELES BALLERS
2018
↓
ILLAWARRA HAWKS
2019–2020
↓
CHARLOTTE HORNETS
2020–PRESENT

NBA DRAFT

2020
1ST ROUND
3RD OVERALL PICK

TROPHY CABINET

NBA ALL-STAR	X1
NBA ROOKIE OF THE YEAR	X1
NBA ALL-ROOKIE FIRST TEAM	X1
NBL ROOKIE OF THE YEAR	X1
JBA CHAMPION	X1
JBA ALL-STAR	X1

BIOGRAPHY

BORN	AUG 22, 2001
NATIONALITY	AMERICAN
BIRTHPLACE	ANAHEIM, CALIFORNIA
HEIGHT	6 FT 7 IN (2.01 M)
POSITION(S)	PG

LaMelo Ball is another player who almost prefers to assist his teammates more than take all the points for himself. He is a team player and the man who just beat Anthony Edwards in the voting for the 2020–2021 Rookie of the Year award, as we covered in the previous biography. LaMelo has already been an All-Star, but his journey to reach the NBA is a little different than usual!

LaMelo was born into the famous Ball family on August 22, 2001. His father, LaVar, is a successful businessman whose dream has always been to raise superstar kids. Chicago Bulls point guard Lonzo Ball and Greensboro Swarm's shooting guard LiAngelo Ball are both LaMelo's brothers. LaVar also founded* the Junior Basketball Association (JBA), which he hoped would help mold his sons into top players.

LaMelo, like his brothers, was given a basketball from the moment he could hold one. At 4, he began playing with his two older brothers, absorbing every bit of advice they gave him. He was also a fantastic flag football player but only played for fun. Basketball was and is his passion.

His brothers also played alongside him in high school for a short period. During LaMelo's freshman year, there was a slight crossover in age groups, and he shared a court with Lonzo and LiAngelo! With the three Balls together, Chino High School had an insane team. LaMelo scored 27 points on his high school debut, and later in the year, he scored 26 points in a win over Sierra Canyon. This second game was important as the victory clinched the California Interscholastic Federation Southern Section Open Division title.

At the end of his first year, Chino High School had a 35–0 record!

LaMelo's first taste of fame came on December 26, 2016, when he was just 15. Two seconds into a Chino High School game, he made a half-court shot that went viral! A couple of months later, he was in the news again when he finally suffered his first high school loss after a 60-game winning streak! That's right—LaMelo was halfway through his freshman year before his first defeat!

He didn't let the disappointment of losing his first game bother him for too long. In fact, he took it out on his very next opponents, scoring an incredible 92 points in a dominant victory over Los Osos High School, the second-most single-game points in California high school history!

LaMelo was considered a five-star recruit, but instead of waiting for college, he decided to cut his high school career short and travel overseas to play professionally. This is almost unheard of in American sports, but the Balls have never done things the so-called normal way. Alongside his older brother LiAngelo, LaMelo signed for Lithuanian team BC Prienai, making him the youngest basketball player in history to sign a pro contract.

His time in Lithuania wasn't the best, though. The coach didn't give him as many minutes on the court as he had expected, and he returned to America soon after. He signed for the Los Angeles Ballers, a team owned and run by his father. They played in his father's JBA league, and LaMelo was seen as the face of the company. It was a lot of pressure for a kid who was yet to turn 18.

LaMelo posted a triple-double on his debut (40 points, 16 rebounds, and 10 assists) and then followed it up with seven more in a row before the season ended. By the 2020 Draft, LaMelo felt he was ready to make the giant leap into the NBA. He was selected third overall by the Charlotte Hornets, but things didn't go as smoothly as he had planned.

LaMelo's preseason was average at best, which meant that he would start the regular season on the bench. For a player who grew up being the main man on every team he played for, it was tough to take. He made his NBA debut on December 23, 2020, playing a scoreless 16 minutes in a 121–114 loss to the Cleveland Cavaliers.

His breakout game came a couple of weeks later against the New Orleans Pelicans, which was made even more special by the fact that he was facing his brother Lonzo for the first time as an NBA player! With the Hornets 18 points down and time running out, LaMelo led the team to a 118–110 victory. He just narrowly missed out on his first triple-double, putting up 12 points, 10 rebounds, and nine assists.

He did manage to get his first triple-double the following day when he hit 22 points, 12 rebounds, and 11 assists in a 113–105 win over the Atlanta Hawks. It meant LaMelo was the youngest player in NBA history to record a triple-double at just 19 years and 140 days old. Amazingly, he still hadn't started a game yet!

That day came on February 1, 2021, as the Hornets beat the Miami Heat 129–121. LaMelo finished the game with 14 points, five rebounds, and seven assists. Four days later, he scored a then-career-high 34 points, becoming the youngest player in history to score 30-plus points in a single game.

He was named Rookie of the Year at the end of his first season. The following season, he was named to his first NBA All-Star Game. His rise was rapid!

The 2022–23 season was a disappointment. Several injuries throughout the year meant he couldn't find any rhythm, and then the season was cut short when he fractured his ankle on February 27 during a win over the Pistons. Still, it wasn't all bad. A while before that, he had become the second-youngest player in NBA history to reach 1,000 points, 1,000 rebounds, and 1,000 assists!

He returned for the 2023–24 season ready to rock, and after signing a new massive contract with the Hornets, he began with a 30-point, 13-assist, 10-rebound triple-double against the Dallas Mavericks!

The Charlotte Hornets have never won an NBA Championship or even a conference title, but with LaMelo leading the team, there is a good chance history will soon be made! LaMelo Ball is a born superstar who had millions of social media followers and subscribers long before he even made it to the NBA. He could be just the thing the Hornets need to reach the top!

JAREN
JACKSON JR.

CAREER

MEMPHIS GRIZZLIES
2018–PRESENT

NBA DRAFT
2018
1ST ROUND
4TH OVERALL PICK

TROPHY CABINET

NBA ALL–STAR	**X1**
NBA DEFENSIVE PLAYER OF THE YEAR	**X1**
NBA ALL–DEFENSIVE FIRST TEAM	**X2**
NBA ALL–ROOKIE FIRST TEAM	**X1**
NBA BLOCKS LEADER	**X2**
BIG TEN DEFENSIVE PLAYER OF THE YEAR	**X1**

BIOGRAPHY

BORN	SEP 15, 1999
NATIONALITY	AMERICAN
BIRTHPLACE	PLAINFIELD, NEW JERSEY
HEIGHT	6 FT 10 IN (2.08 M)
POSITION(S)	C / PF

With unbelievable reflexes and great anticipation, Jaren Jackson Jr.'s defensive skill set makes the power forward and center one of the hardest guys any opponent will face. Every team needs someone like "JJJ" on their roster if they want to be successful. It is these types of players that carry the weight so the more attacking players can shine.

Jaren Jackson Jr. was born in Plainfield, New Jersey, on September 15, 1999. Right from the start, he was surrounded by basketball. His father, Jaren, was an NBA player and coach, while his mother, Terri, is an executive director of the Women's National Basketball Players Association. It was kind of written in the stars that JJJ would become an NBA player!

Jaren attended Park Tudor School in Indianapolis, and he was an instant hit with the team. His defensive skills and ability to see the play unfold from deep was priceless, but he could also score, averaging 10 points per game. In his time at Park Tudor, he won two Indiana High School Athletic Association State Championships as he formed a devastating partnership with future professional player Trevon Bluiett.

Jaren was considered one of the best prospects in his 2017 class by the time he graduated and ranked fifth overall by Scout.com. They also ranked him the best in his position. He played in the McDonald's All-American Game on March 29, 2017, and by the summer, he was on the radar of almost every top college in the country.

JJJ didn't think about the rest. He had made his decision to enroll in Michigan State long before he graduated. Michigan's team was run by Hall of Famer coach Tom Izzo, and Jaren wanted to play under him. As he has done all through his career, Jaren wanted to push himself to his limit.

His college debut couldn't have gone any better. Jaren recorded 13 points and an insane 13 rebounds as Michigan smashed North Florida 98–66. The team lost the next game to number-one-ranked Duke, but JJJ was still superb, putting up 19 points while impressing with his defensive talents.

By the end of the regular season, he was named Big Ten Defensive Player of the Year and Freshman of the Year. This led to his decision to finish college early and declare for the NBA Draft while he was hot. It worked, and the Memphis Grizzlies selected him with the fourth overall pick.

His NBA career took off quickly, and in December of his rookie season, he put up 43 points in a 127–114 loss to the Milwaukee Bucks. His nine three-pointers in that game tied him with the franchise record. He was already adored by the Grizzlies' fans.

JJJ's defensive talents were on full display on January 28, 2020, when he recorded seven blocks as the Grizzlies beat the Nuggets 104–96. He continued his fine form right up until August when he tore his meniscus* in a game against the New Orleans Pelicans. The injury kept him out for the rest of the 2019–2020 season. It was so bad that it would keep him out until April 2021.

When he finally did return, JJJ picked up where he had left off, recording an impressive 15 points, eight rebounds, and four blocks against the Los Angeles Clippers. Two days later, he put up 23 points as the team beat the Portland Trail Blazers. With Jaren back on the team, the Grizzlies suddenly caught fire, and several wins in a row set them up for their first playoff appearance in four years!

Unfortunately, the Grizzlies met the Utah Jazz, who were the top seed. The Grizzlies lost in five games, but the team was clearly on the rise, which was proven when they reached the playoffs again the following season.

This time, the Grizzlies progressed, beating the Timberwolves in an epic series that saw JJJ set a franchise record for blocks in a playoff game. They came up against the Golden State Warriors in Round 2, with Jaren putting up 33 points in Game 1. He added 10 rebounds to that but couldn't stop the Grizzlies from losing the game by a single point. The Warriors won the series before going on to win the NBA Championship.

Jaren finished the 2021–22 season with more blocks than anyone else. In fact, it wasn't even close—he had 40 more blocks than the guy in second place! He was named to the NBA All-Defensive First Team, yet somehow only finished fifth in the Defensive Player of the Year voting.

More injuries affected his 2022–23 season, and he missed the opening 14 games after surgery to help heal a fractured foot. He returned on November 15 in a 113–102 loss to the New Orleans Pelicans, and his form was soon back to his best. A few weeks later, JJJ recorded 15 points, eight blocks, and seven rebounds as the Grizzlies beat the Hawks 128–103.

Against the Orlando Magic in early 2023, Jaren put in one of the best performances of his young career when he dominated his opponents throughout the game. He put up 31 points, 10 rebounds, and three blocks in a 123–115 win. A month later, he was selected to his first All-Star Game.

The Grizzlies reached the playoffs again, this time losing in six games to the Lakers. JJJ was named Defensive Player of the Year for the first time and to the All-Defensive First Team for the second. On a personal level, it was a very successful season, but Jaren is a team player, and until the Grizzlies win the NBA Championship, he'll never be satisfied!

The Grizzlies' fans believe that Jaren Jackson Jr. is the type of player to build the franchise around, and they're not wrong. As mentioned earlier, every successful team needs a JJJ-type player to be the best. Jaren will surely get his chance to play in the NBA Finals one day. When he does, you can be sure he'll give it his all!

RHYNE HOWARD

CAREER

ATLANTA DREAM
2022-PRESENT
↓
BERETTA FAMILA SCHIO
2022-2023

WNBA DRAFT

2022
1ST ROUND
1ST PICK OVERALL

TROPHY CABINET

WNBA ROOKIE OF THE YEAR	X1
WNBA ALL-STAR	X2
WNBA ALL-ROOKIE TEAM	X1
FIRST-TEAM ALL-AMERICAN	X3
SEC PLAYER OF THE YEAR	X2
SEC TOURNAMENT MVP	X1
FIRST-TEAM ALL-SEC	X4

BIOGRAPHY

BORN	APRIL 29, 2000
NATIONALITY	AMERICAN
BIRTHPLACE	CHATTANOOGA, TENNESSEE
HEIGHT	6 FT 2 IN (1.88 M)
POSITION(S)	G

Rhyne Howard is one of those players who could do well in any position. She can do everything on the court—score, assist, rebound, and defend. You name it, she can do it! Her height will always give her an advantage, but she is also a leader. It would be no surprise at all if she becomes a successful coach when her playing days are over. Her knowledge of the game is scary!

Rhyne is one of the slightly older players on our list. Born in Chattanooga, Tennessee, on April 29, 2000, she grew up in a loving family, which helped when she began being bullied in school because of her height. But like a lot of the people on this list, she did everything she could to turn a negative into a positive. She fought back, using her time on the courts to show the other kids just how good she was at basketball.

Sadly, whenever she wasn't on the court, Rhyne was cripplingly shy. Her years in high school were spent with her head held low as she struggled to come out of her shell. She stuck it out, though, and the small circle of friends she made became extra tight!

As hard as high school can be for the kids who don't fit in, college is where the very same people who struggled become popular. Kids spend their teenage years trying to be the same as everybody else, and then around the time they hit college age, everyone suddenly wants to be different! Rhyne shed her shyness at the University of Kentucky and began to show how amazing she was, both on and off the court.

But that all came after high school. Despite her shyness, Rhyne excelled in both sports and academics while still at Bradley Central. She made waves early when she was named 2018 Tennessee Gatorade Player of the Year and Tennessee Miss Basketball in 2018. On top of that, she starred at the FIBA Under-18 Women's AmeriCup, helping the USA win gold!

All of this led to her being named to the Jordan Brand Classic, a yearly game between the hottest prospects in American basketball. By the time she graduated, she was being chased by most of the top colleges. As we know, she chose Kentucky, where she would go on to star for the Wildcats.

Rhyne spent four years at the University of Kentucky, winning SEC Player of the Year honors in both 2020 and 2021. She also earned SEC All-Defensive Team and SEC First Team honors. By the time she finished with the Wildcats, she was the only player in the country averaging 19 points and 7.5 rebounds per game. She also recorded 40 steals and 70 assists in that time!

She was one of the country's hottest prospects going into the 2022 WNBA Draft. She was selected first overall by the Atlanta Dream and picked up where she had left off with the Wildcats, averaging 16.8 points, 2.8 assists, and 1.6 steals throughout the season. Amazingly, she started every game of her rookie season!

In an incredible first year with the Dream, Rhyne somehow won Rookie of the Month four times in a row between May and August. She was named to her first All-Star Game in July, and she ended the season as WNBA Rookie of the Year. That All-Star selection was the first of three in a row, and it's safe to say she will make it four in a row pretty soon!

Like many women's players, Rhyne has to split her time between her WNBA team and one in Europe. She moved to Italy for the 2022–2023 Serie A* season, where she played for Beretta Famila Schio. She's as popular there as she is with the Dream's fans!

After winning the FIBA Under-19 Women's AmeriCup in 2019, Rhyne flew out to Puerto Rico with the senior team in 2021, hoping to bring home the gold again. She was phenomenal throughout, finishing with the MVP award as America won the tournament. They beat the hosts in the Final, and Rhyne had another gold medal to hang around her neck!

She was part of the proud American athletes that traveled to Paris for the 2024 Olympic Games. Alongside Hailey Van Lith, Cierra Burdick, and Dearica Hamby, Rhyne competed on the 3x3 Women's Basketball team. After being shocked by Spain in the Semifinals, the team picked themselves up to win the bronze after beating Canada 16–13.

Even though they didn't win gold, Team USA's 3x3 Women's team caught the nation's imagination. Soon after returning from Paris, a new national 3x3 league was announced, with Rhyne agreeing to play in the inaugural* season!

Rhyne has been so popular in her short time with the Dream that the era from 2022—when she signed—to the present is being hailed as the Rhyne Howard Era! The Dream made huge changes to try to bring success, hiring Tanisha Wright as head coach and announcing new big-time partners such as Xbox and Microsoft. It's hoped that Tanisha Wright and Rhyne Howard can be the duo to lead the team to success.

The Dream lost in the 2023 playoffs to the Dallas Wings, but major improvements could be seen throughout the season. Now that Tanisha and Rhyne have had a chance to gel, it should only be a matter of time before the WNBA feels the full force of the Dream!

Rhyne Howard is one of those one-in-a-million type of players. They don't come along often, but when they do, just be glad you were around to witness their brilliance!

PAOLO
BANCHERO

CAREER

ORLANDO MAGIC
2022–PRESENT

NBA DRAFT

2022
1ST ROUND
1ST OVERALL PICK

TROPHY CABINET

NBA ALL-STAR	X1
NBA ROOKIE OF THE YEAR	X1
NBA ALL-ROOKIE FIRST TEAM	X1
CONSENSUS SECOND TEAM ALL-AMERICAN	X1
FIRST-TEAM ALL-ACC	X1
ACC ROOKIE OF THE YEAR	X1
ACC ALL-FRESHMAN TEAM	X1

BIOGRAPHY

BORN	NOV 12, 2002
NATIONALITY	AMERICAN / ITALIAN
BIRTHPLACE	SEATTLE, WASHINGTON
HEIGHT	6 FT 10 IN (2.08 M)
POSITION(S)	PF

Paolo Banchero is a bit of a blast from the past. His back-to-the-basket style looks like something from the 1990s, yet his speed and epic bank shots are completely modern. He's a mix of the best of both worlds!

Born in Seattle, Washington, on November 12, 2002, Paolo Banchero is another of our future stars who grew up surrounded by basketball. His mother, Rhonda, played college ball at Washington, finishing her time there as the program's all-time leading scorer. She was a third-round selection for the 2000 WNBA Draft, but her potential was never really reached, and she became a coach soon after.

Paolo's father and uncle were also successful college players, so he was never short of advice and training techniques.

One of the most amazing things about Paolo is that he was three feet tall at just 15 months old! Yep, you read that right—he was the size of an average 4-year-old boy when he was still a toddler!

Paolo attended O'Dea High School, where he fell in love with organized basketball. Unlike most kids, his basketball hero wasn't an NBA star. No, it was his mother! In addition to basketball, Paolo was also a fantastic football player and track athlete.

By sixth grade, Paolo was six foot one, and the following year, he hit six foot five. In his first year at O'Dea, he was part of the basketball, football, and track teams. As backup quarterback for the football team, he helped O'Dea to the state championship, but his true passion was on the courts. He averaged 14.1 points and 10 rebounds per game as a freshman and then 18.2 and 10.3 as a sophomore. As a junior, his stats rose even higher.

Paolo was named to the McDonald's All-American Game as his high school career came to an end, and he was considered a consensus five-star recruit. Several NCAA Division I colleges chased him, and he was expected to choose his mother and father's college, the University of Washington. So, it was a huge shock when he decided on Duke University!

His decision proved correct, and his college career started perfectly. He scored 22 points on his debut in a 79–71 win against Kentucky, and his early performances earned him his first Atlantic Coast Conference (ACC) Freshman of the Week honor. Two weeks later, he won it again! His form continued, and he was named ACC Rookie of the Year at the end of his first season.

After such a successful rookie year at Duke, Paolo decided he was ready for the NBA and declared himself for the 2022 Draft. He was selected with the first overall pick by the Orlando Magic, which came as a shock, as the Magic had put a lot of scouting into Jaren Jackson Jr. As we know, JJJ went to the Memphis Grizzlies, but it's fair to say that both franchises won in the 2022 NBA Draft!

Paolo's regular season debut came on October 19 against the Detroit Pistons. He recorded an impressive 27 points, nine rebounds, five assists, and two blocks, even with the team losing 113–109. Still, his brilliant numbers made him the first debutant since LeBron James to put up at least 25 points, five rebounds, and five assists in the NBA!

The team continued to struggle, but Paolo kept improving. He scored 33 points and 16 rebounds as the Magic lost to the Sacramento Kings, making him the second teenager in NBA history after LeBron James (again!) to score 30 points and 15 rebounds in a game!

Despite the Magic not performing very well, Paolo still won Rookie of the Year, which only proves how amazing he was that season. It's much harder to win individual honors in a team that's struggling.

By the 2023–2024 season, the rest of the team was starting to come up to Paolo's standard. In a game against the Utah Jazz in early November, Paolo contributed 30 points and the game-winning layup in a 115–113 win. Two days later, he recorded a double-double as the Magic beat the Los Angeles Lakers.

January saw his first triple-double—30 points, 10 rebounds, and 11 assists—as the Magic overcame the Nuggets. Paolo's and the team's improvement meant that the Magic reached the playoffs as division champions, which was a huge step up from the previous season.

The Magic came up against the Cleveland Cavaliers in Round 1, with Paolo again showing how good he was as he stood out in the series. He recorded 39 points, eight rebounds, and four assists in Game 5, yet the Magic still lost the game by a single point. He did even better in Game 7, but he couldn't stop the Magic from losing a nail-biting series.

Paolo almost played for Italy in 2022. His father is Italian, and he considered an international career playing for his father's homeland. But his loyalty to his mother won out, and he declared for the USA just before Italy competed in their 2022 EuroBasket qualifiers. The Italian fans have never forgiven him for getting their hopes up!

Paolo Banchero is a superb prospect. His rookie season, when he had to carry the rest of the team at times, has helped him mature much quicker than usual. That can only be a good thing, as he has the on-court knowledge of a much more experienced player. With the Magic constantly improving alongside him, there is every chance that they will soon be major contenders. Until then, the team's fans can just sit back and enjoy watching one of the hottest prospects in the NBA!

ZION
WILLIAMSON

CAREER

NEW ORLEANS PELICANS
2019–PRESENT

NBA DRAFT
2019
1ST ROUND
1ST OVERALL PICK

TROPHY CABINET

NBA ALL–STAR	X2
NBA ALL–ROOKIE FIRST TEAM	X1
NATIONAL COLLEGE PLAYER OF THE YEAR	X1
CONSENSUS FIRST TEAM ALL–AMERICAN	X1
WAYMAN TISDALE AWARD	X1
ACC PLAYER OF THE YEAR	X1

BIOGRAPHY

BORN	**JULY 6, 2000**
NATIONALITY	**AMERICAN**
BIRTHPLACE	SALISBURY, NORTH CAROLINA
HEIGHT	6 FT 6 IN (1.98 M)
POSITION(S)	PF

An explosive power forward with electric dunking ability, Zion Williamson is one of the most devastating young talents in the NBA right now. His injury problems have held him back a little, but even so, he has already made a name for himself as an essential part of the New Orleans Pelicans team.

Born in Salisbury, North Carolina, on July 6, 2000, Zion showed signs of being a top athlete at an early age. His father, Lateef, was a brilliant defensive lineman at Mayo High School and a High School All-American in 1993. His mother was also athletic, and she was a superb sprinter in her youth. When she got older, she became a physical education teacher, so Zion always had a motivation to excel in sports.

When Zion was 2, his family moved to Florence, South Carolina, and when he was 5, his parents divorced. His mother soon married a man named Lee Anderson, who had been a successful college basketball player. Lee inspired Zion to play basketball and also helped him practice.

It was around this time that Zion started making claims that he would one day play in the NBA. Most people laughed, as he was just a kid, but his parents knew he had what it took. At the age of 9, Zion was waking himself up at 5 a.m. to go running and to train. His dedication to being the best is something that has helped set him apart from the rest over the years.

He attended Spartanburg Day School, a small K-12* private school in South Carolina. Between the eighth and ninth grades, he grew from five foot nine to six foot three, and by the summer of his freshman year, he was already able to dunk! This skill would become one of his trademarks as he got older.

During this period, he also played for the South Carolina Hornets AAU team, where he was a teammate of Ja Morant! Then, in August 2015, he won the Under Armour Elite 24 showcase dunk contest in New York. It was the first time he really came to the attention of the public, which can sometimes make or break a player, especially when they're young. Thankfully, Zion has always shone brightest under the spotlight!

Zion was offered his first college scholarship while he was still a freshman, and by the time he finished high school, 16 NCAA Division I colleges were chasing him! He was a five-star recruit and ranked the number one player in the country in the 2018 class by 247 Sports. After considering all of his options, he chose Duke, like so many other great prospects.

He played 23 minutes in his college debut, scoring 28 points on 11-of-13 shooting. Before long, Zion was breaking records at Duke left, right, and center! Everything seemed perfect until a freak injury when his Nike sneaker ripped open 36 seconds into a game against North Carolina. When the sneaker burst open, Zion injured his ankle, and it didn't look good. The game was televised, and the shock of how easily the sneaker had fallen apart caused Nike to lose a billion dollars in sales overnight!

Zion missed six games before returning with 29 points, 14 rebounds, and five steals in an 84–72 win over Syracuse in the Quarterfinals of the ACC tournament. Duke lost the Final to North Carolina by a single point, but Zion was still named tournament MVP.

By the 2019 season, Zion was national news. CBS dedicated a camera to follow him throughout each game, which became known as Zion Cam! The pressure was insane, but Zion handled it like a boss, putting in several MVP performances. At the end of the season, he declared himself for the 2019 NBA Draft.

The Pelicans drafted him with the first overall pick, and he officially signed on July 1, 2019. Sadly, he tore his meniscus a few months later, which pretty much ruined a huge chunk of his rookie season. He finally made his pro debut three months later in a 121–77 loss to the Spurs. He only managed 18 minutes, yet somehow recorded 22 points and seven rebounds in that time!

He quickly made up for lost time, scoring at least 20 points in each of his next eight games. By the end of this run, he had more consecutive 20-plus point games than any other teenager in the history of the NBA! He finished the season as the first rookie since Michael Jordan to post 16 20-point games in their first 20 games. He was named NBA All-Rookie First Team despite missing a huge portion of the season.

His 20-point game records continued the following

season, and he tied the legendary Kareem Abdul-Jabbar for the longest streak of at least 20 points per game in their first two seasons. The streak eventually rose to 25 games, meaning he passed Hall of Famers Wilt Chamberlain and Karl Malone. It also tied him with Shaquille O'Neal.

Zion suffered another injury during the offseason, this time a fractured foot that required surgery. At first, it was believed he would be fit in time for the regular season, but several setbacks meant that he ended up missing the whole thing! Still, he had already done enough to let the Pelicans know that he was irreplaceable, and he signed a massive contract in 2022.

He made his return a few months after signing his new deal, putting up 13 points, four rebounds, and one assist in a 129–125 preseason win over the Chicago Bulls. On his regular season return, he recorded 25 points, nine rebounds, three assists, and four steals as the Pelicans beat the Brooklyn Nets 130–108.

Right after being named the Western Conference Player of the Week in early January 2023, Zion injured his hamstring. Again, his recovery took much longer than expected, and he missed the rest of the season. It also meant that he couldn't play in his second All-Star Game. So many setbacks would be a lot for anyone to take, and Zion is only human, after all. He could be forgiven for feeling like he has rotten luck. Thankfully for Pelicans' fans, he's a fighter, and he always comes back stronger than ever.

Off the court, Zion is known for his generosity. During

the COVID-19 pandemic, he paid the salaries of all the employees of the Smoothie King Center for a whole month!

Meanwhile, on the court, Zion has already become one of the most feared power forwards in the NBA. Injuries have kept him from truly blossoming, but despite these setbacks, he somehow continues to improve each year. If he gets a run of seasons without any major injuries, Zion could easily become one of the Pelicans' greatest-ever players!

FRANZ
WAGNER

CAREER

ALBA BERLIN
2017–2019
↓
SSV LOKOMOTIVE BERNAU
2018–2019
↓
ORLANDO MAGIC
2021–PRESENT

NBA DRAFT
2021
1ST ROUND
8TH OVERALL PICK

TROPHY CABINET

NBA ALL-ROOKIE FIRST TEAM	X1
SECOND-TEAM ALL-BIG TEN	X1
THIRD-TEAM ALL-BIG TEN	X1
BUNDESLIGA BEST GERMAN YOUNG PLAYER	X1
FIRST-TEAM ACADEMIC ALL-AMERICAN	X1

BIOGRAPHY

BORN	AUG 27, 2001
NATIONALITY	GERMAN
BIRTHPLACE	BERLIN
HEIGHT	6 FT 10 IN (2.08 M)
POSITION(S)	SF

Another small forward and a player who has become Paolo Banchero's understudy* at the Orlando Magic, Franz Wagner has the potential to be one of the best. His athleticism is phenomenal for such a big guy, and when added to his shooting ability, it makes for one dangerous player.

Franz Wagner was born in Berlin, Germany, on August 27, 2001. He is the younger brother of Moritz Wagner, who recently (at the time of the book being written) joined Franz at Orlando Magic. Like his brother, Franz was a natural from the moment he first held a ball, and together, they dominated the local Berlin courts growing up.

After being chased by most of the top European clubs, Franz decided to stay in his hometown and sign for Alba Berlin. He was fast-tracked* through the youth ranks and made his professional debut at just 16! At this point, he was already six foot five!

Even as Franz was making his pro debut, he was still in high school. His love of basketball never got in the way of his studies, and he was so smart that he skipped a grade. After earning his diploma, he threw everything into basketball practice and soon became Alba Berlin's main player.

Franz won gold with Germany at the Albert Schweitzer

Tournament in 2018, and a year later, he was named the best young player in Germany. Alba Berlin (and most of the best European teams) tried to convince him to sign up with them, but Franz knew he was ready for the NBA. He packed his bags and flew over to the States to start his college career!

Considered a four-star recruit, Franz was chased by several NCAA Division I programs. In the end, he chose Michigan mainly because he would get to train under coach Juwan Howard. Unfortunately, Franz fractured his wrist soon after enrolling, which meant he missed the first few months of his freshman season. Being such a determined player, this time off the courts must have killed him.

He made his college debut on November 27, 2019, recording six points, three rebounds, and one block in 23 minutes. A week later, he put up 18 points in a 103–91 win over Iowa. Not long after, Franz recorded his first double-double for Michigan in a loss to Ohio State. Many brilliant performances followed, which led to him being named to the 2020 Big Ten All-Freshman team.

Franz's freshman year was good, but his sophomore season was even better. Having impressed with his agility and grace, his scoring dramatically improved as the new season progressed. On top of 14 double-figure games and four 20-plus point games, he also recorded the most steals on the team (30) and the second-most blocks (23). After such an outstanding sophomore year, Franz decided to cut his college time short and declare for the NBA Draft.

He was selected eighth overall by the Orlando Magic, who also snapped up Jalen Suggs in a very successful 2021 Draft.

After edging his way onto the Magic team, Franz's NBA career really took off on December 18, when he recorded his first double-double. A couple of weeks later, he put up 38 points in a 127–110 loss to the Milwaukee Bucks. His performances throughout that December saw him win Rookie of the Month.

Franz didn't take his foot off the gas in January, and he recorded another double-double, posting 14 points and 10 assists. It made him the first rookie in Magic history to record 10 assists in an NBA game. He was quickly becoming an important team player and someone the Magic could depend on in big games.

He finished his first season with the Orlando Magic as part of the NBA All-Rookie First Team!

One of his proudest moments came at the 2023 FIBA Basketball World Cup when he won gold with Germany! It was the first time Germany had ever won the World Cup, and to make it even more special, Franz did it alongside his brother and teammate, Moritz!

The Magic finished the 2023–2024 season as division champions, where they came up against the Cleveland Cavaliers in the first round. In Game 4 of the series, Franz recorded 34 points on 13-of-17 shooting, as well as 13 rebounds in a 112–89 victory to tie the series at 2–2. In the end, the Magic lost a squeaker in seven games, but the progress of the team was there for all to see.

With young players such as Franz, Paolo Banchero, Jalen Suggs, and Jett Howard on their roster, the Orlando Magic are one of the most promising teams in the NBA. If they can hold on to all of this amazing talent, who knows how many NBA Championships they can win in the future!

Franz Wagner made his professional debut at 16 and has gone from strength to strength every year since. He's already a World Cup winner and was an important part of the Orlando Magic team that reached the 2024 playoffs as division champions. The sky really is the limit for the small forward from Berlin.

VICTOR
WEMBANYAMA

CAREER

NANTERRE 92
2019–2021
↓
ASVEL
2021–2022
↓
METROPOLITANS 92
2022–2023
↓
SAN ANTONIO SPURS
2023–PRESENT

TROPHY CABINET

NBA ROOKIE OF THE YEAR	X1
NBA ALL-DEFENSIVE FIRST TEAM	X1
NBA ALL-ROOKIE FIRST TEAM	X1
NBA BLOCKS LEADER	X1

NBA DRAFT

2023
1ST ROUND
1ST OVERALL PICK

BIOGRAPHY

BORN	JAN 4, 2004
NATIONALITY	FRENCH
BIRTHPLACE	LE CHESNAY
HEIGHT	7 FT 4 IN (2.24 M)
POSITION(S)	C / PF

At seven foot four, Victor Wembanyama has somehow managed to be one of the most nimble young players in the NBA while also maintaining his brute strength. He handles and shoots like a guard, and his height makes his jump shot nearly impossible to block. He almost single-handedly carried France to the Final at the 2024 Olympics, only to lose to the USA in the fourth quarter. Still, silver at the Olympics is a brilliant achievement for any player, and Victor is young enough to play again at the 2028 Olympic Games!

Victor Wembanyama was born in Le Chesnay, France, on January 4, 2004. His father was a superb athlete who competed in the long jump, triple jump, and high jump, while his mother is a former basketball player and current coach. Both of his parents are tall—his father is six foot six, and his mother is six foot three—so it's no surprise that Victor grew to be the joint-tallest player currently playing in the NBA!

All of the Wembanyama kids excelled in sports. His younger brother is a brilliant handball player, and his sister plays basketball professionally. Victor also loved soccer and judo as a kid, and it is said that he could have been a top goalkeeper had he continued with soccer. Thankfully for the San Antonio Spurs, he decided to concentrate on basketball.

Victor was spotted playing basketball young, and after

being scouted, he was signed by Nanterre 92 when he was just 10. It didn't take him long to impress his coaches, and by the age of 15, he was thrown into a EuroCup game, making him the second-youngest player in the tournament's history! He continued to play for the Under-16 and Under-18 teams while still appearing for the senior team from time to time.

By the 2020–21 season, he was not only a regular on the senior team but the hottest prospect in the country. At 17, he moved to ASVEL of the Pro A league* but fell ill soon after and didn't play for several months. When he finally made his ASVEL debut on October 1, 2021, the fans packed the arena to see the hottest prospect in French sport. Sadly, a few weeks later, he fractured his finger, and he was held back for another couple of months.

His time at ASVEL continued like that, with injuries constantly stalling his progress. He signed for Metropolitans 92 on July 4, 2022, as he wanted to play under coach Vincent Collet, who was famous for helping players reach their full potential.

A life-changing moment came when Victor took part in two exhibition games against the NBA G League Ignite, which were shown on TVs all over the States. There were 200 NBA scouts in the crowd looking to spot new talent, and in the first game, Victor recorded 37 points, five blocks, and four rebounds. In the second game, he recorded 36 points and 11 rebounds. His performances were so good that ESPN announced they would show the rest of Metropolitans 92's games that season so fans in the USA could keep up with Victor's progress!

The 2022–2023 season saw Victor emerge as one of the best players in Europe despite still being so young. At the Ligue Nationale de Basket (LNB) All-Star Game, he put up 27 points, 12 rebounds, and four assists. He was awarded the game's MVP, becoming the youngest player in history to do so. He could have stayed on in Europe and signed for any team he wanted, but he couldn't be held back any longer. The call of the NBA was too strong!

Victor was selected first overall by the San Antonio Spurs. He is the only French player in NBA history to be drafted first overall and only the second European after Andrea Bargnani in 2006. It's hard to remember a time when there was more excitement about an NBA Draft selection.

He made his NBA regular season debut on October 25, 2023, recording 15 points, five rebounds, and two blocks in a 126–119 loss to the Dallas Mavericks. He hit three three-pointers, which is a franchise record for a rookie. It made him an instant favorite of the Mavericks' fans. They loved him even more when he put up 38 points, 10 rebounds, and two blocks a week later in a 132–121 victory over the Suns.

On December 8, 2023, he became the youngest player to record 21 points and 20 rebounds in a single game, but he couldn't stop the Spurs from losing to the Bulls. Victor was still just 19. Two days later, after consecutive double-doubles, he hit a triple-double of 16 points, 12 rebounds, and 10 assists in a 130–108 win over the Detroit Pistons. He did it again a month later (27 points, 14 rebounds, and 10 blocks) as the Spurs beat the Toronto Raptors.

If people thought things couldn't get any better for Victor, they were wrong. On February 23, 2024, he became the youngest player in NBA history to put up a 5x5 when he recorded 27 points, 10 rebounds, eight assists, five steals, and five blocks against the Lakers. What is truly amazing about this is that he did it in just 30 minutes!

At the end of his rookie season, Victor led the league in blocks (3.6 per game), making him the youngest player in history to do so. His performances throughout the year were outstanding, and it's clear that the Spurs have a future legend on their roster. He became only the sixth player in NBA history to be unanimously voted Rookie of the Year.

Victor isn't just big in size; he is big in personality too. He's a superstar, and what makes him special is that he doesn't seem to notice the pressure. His cool nature helps him to dominate on the court, while his height and natural grace make it nearly impossible for opponents to hold him back. If he keeps improving at the same rate, there is no limit to how successful he can become.

Victor Wembanyama is an Olympian, a unanimous Rookie of the Year, and the holder of several NBA records. He is playing for a team with potential, and he is adored by the fans. His highlight reel is already insane, and his passion to always be better drives him on. Remember the name because Victor Wembanyama could be one of the greatest players of his generation!

JALEN
WILLIAMS

CAREER

**OKLAHOMA
CITY
THUNDER**
2022–PRESENT

NBA DRAFT

2022
1ST ROUND
12TH OVERALL PICK

TROPHY CABINET

NBA ALL-ROOKIE
FIRST TEAM   X1

FIRST TEAM ALL-WCC   X1

BIOGRAPHY

BORN	APRIL 14, 2001
NATIONALITY	AMERICAN
BIRTHPLACE	DENVER, COLORADO
HEIGHT	6 FT 5 IN (1.96 M)
POSITION(S)	SF / PF / SG

A tall, smooth, small forward who can score and step in as a brilliant shooting guard, Jalen Williams has only started to be given the respect he deserves. He was seen as decent during high school and good by the time he hit college. After a short time in the NBA, Jalen is now considered one of the best prospects in the country.

Jalen Williams was born in Denver, Colorado, on April 14, 2001. His parents were both in the United States Air Force, which meant that the family moved around a lot. When he was 7, they moved to Arizona, where he attended Perry High School.

Jalen's younger brother, Cody, was also a fantastic player as a kid, and he went on to get drafted by the Utah Jazz in 2023. In fact, Cody could have easily made this list, and don't be surprised if he becomes one of the NBA's better players. Cody was actually a consensus five-star recruit and rated higher than his older brother!

While playing as a point guard at Perry High School, Jalen began getting a name for himself as a dynamic shooter. He was six feet tall in his sophomore year, and then he grew another five inches that summer! Jalen was seen as a pretty good player, but he was only ranked ninth among prep players in Arizona. Although this would be a dream for 99% of people, it's pretty average for an NBA hopeful!

By his junior year, Jalen's reputation had started to grow. He was named the Chandler Unified School District Player of the Year as a junior and the 2017–18 Region Offensive Player of the Year as a senior. All this led to him being rated as a three-star recruit by 247 Sports and Rivals.

Jalen committed to Santa Clara and made his college debut on November 5, 2019, recording 13 points, five rebounds, four assists, and two steals against UC Santa Cruz. After that, he played in all 33 of his freshman games, starting 23 of them! He led the team in steals, which put him third on Santa Clara's all-time list.

During one insane performance against Mississippi Valley State, Jalen had one of those games that seemed superhuman. He recorded his highest points, rebounds, field goals, three-pointers, and assists totals to date! He put up a double-double in the opening round of the 2021 WCC tournament and then continued to improve almost every game.

Jalen's scoring had never been his biggest talent, but by his final year at Santa Clara, it had become one of his strongest points. Jalen has made a habit of constantly working on different aspects of his game. His hard work and determination, combined with his never-say-die* attitude, have also made him a fan favorite wherever he has played.

Jalen declared for the 2022 NBA Draft and was selected 12th overall by the Oklahoma City Thunder, making him the first Santa Clara player to be drafted since 1997. That 2022 Draft was an exceptional one for the Thunder, who had previously selected Chet Holmgren!

What should have been a dream NBA debut became a nightmare six minutes into it when Jalen fractured his right orbital bone* when trying to block a dunk by Jaden McDaniels. He had already managed to score five points in that six minutes, but the injury kept him out for four games.

When he returned from injury, Jalen was only used from the bench for a while. Then, Thunder forward Jeremiah Robinson-Earl suffered an ankle sprain, and Jalen was thrown into the deep end as a full-time starter. He didn't look back!

Soon after, he had his breakout game in the NBA, dragging the Thunder back from a 20-point deficit* with a 27-point haul to beat the Spurs. This had followed several other brilliant performances, and the day after his 27-point rescue of the Thunder, he was named NBA Rookie of the Month.

Jalen put up a career-high 32 points against the Utah Jazz, the team his younger brother would sign for the following year. He recorded 31 points a few games later against the Charlotte Hornets and then continued his impressive form throughout the season. In fact, he became only the third rookie to have three or more games with at least 25 points, five rebounds, and five assists in a single game.

He finished second in the NBA Rookie of the Year voting, which was majorly impressive, seeing as he had been a 12th overall pick!

His sophomore season was just as good, and he scored a career-high 36 points in a 129–120 win against the New York Knicks. Alongside Chet Holmgren, Jalen helped the Thunder win the division title and then a sweep of New Orleans in Round 1 of the playoffs. As we know from Chet Holmgren's biography, the Dallas Mavericks shocked the Thunder in the Semifinals.

The Oklahoma City Thunder have one of the best young rosters in the NBA. Future stars such as Chet Holmgren, Jalen Williams, and (wait for it!) Jaylin Williams (no relation to this Jalen!) can only mean the future is bright for the team. They might have been upset by the Dallas Mavericks in the playoffs, but they won the division title before that, so we know they're good. The team is surely set to go further very soon!

Jalen William's success in the NBA is special because he wasn't a five-star recruit. Throughout history, some of the NBA's best players weren't highly rated as kids, but their hard work and need to be the best can be the extra bit of stardust needed to make them reach the top. Jalen has improved every season since his freshman year at Perry High School. The same can be said for his time in college and his rapid progress in the NBA. If he keeps stepping up his game at the same rate, we could be looking at a future Hall of Famer!

JALEN GREEN

CAREER

NBA G
LEAGUE
IGNITE
2020-2021
↓
HOUSTON
ROCKETS
2021-PRESENT

NBA DRAFT

2021
1ST ROUND
2ND OVERALL PICK

TROPHY CABINET

NBA ALL-ROOKIE FIRST TEAM	X1
MCDONALD'S ALL-AMERICAN	X1
FIBA UNDER-17 WORLD CUP MVP	X1

BIOGRAPHY

BORN	FEB 9, 2002
NATIONALITY	AMERICAN
BIRTHPLACE	MERCED, CALIFORNIA
HEIGHT	6 FT 4 IN (1.93 M)
POSITION(S)	SG

Time for another Jalen on the list; this time, Jalen Green! In truth, there could have been three Jalens who made our cut, as Jalen Suggs only just missed out.

An almost perfect shooting guard, Jalen Green can assist teammates with ease and attack the rim, and he's been known to get the fans on their feet with his spectacular dunks. He is athletic, quick, and strong, making him a constant danger to opposing teams.

Born in Merced, California, on February 9, 2002, Jalen Green lived in Livingston before moving to Fresno. By the time he was in the sixth grade, he was practicing and training five hours a day. His determination was evident from a very young age. It helped that his stepfather, Marcus, was a fantastic player in his day, having started for Washington Union High School, and he helped influence Jalen to be the best he could be.

Jalen played his first three years of high school basketball at San Joaquin High School in Fresno, where he helped the team to a California Interscholastic Federation (CIF) Central Section runner-up finish in his freshman year. He earned Freshman All-American and Rookie of the Year honors before an even better sophomore season when he averaged 27.9 points and 7.7 rebounds per game.

San Joaquin went one better in Jalen's sophomore year, winning the CIF Section Championships. He was named MaxPreps National Sophomore of the Year. His averages increased again in his junior year—30.1 points, 7.8 rebounds, and 3.6 assists—as he won another Central Division II Championship. If that wasn't enough, he also became the school's all-time leading scorer with 2,288 points.

Jalen represented the United States at the 2018 FIBA Under-17 Basketball World Cup, where the team won gold. The roster included Evan Mobley (coming up later on our list) and Jalen Suggs, to name but a few! Even though he was surrounded by such talent, Jalen Green still managed to get named tournament MVP. Jalen had previously won gold at the Under-16 World Cup, and he would do the same at the Under-19 World Cup as the youngest player on the roster.

Jalen ended his senior year being named All-American Player of the Year by Sports Illustrated, and he was a consensus five-star recruit and number one shooting guard in the 2020 recruiting class. Just about all of the top NCAA Division I programs offered him a scholarship, but Jalen turned them all down. He joined the NBA G League instead, signing a one-year, half-a-million-dollar contract with Ignite. Jalen was one of the first to skip college and join the G League, so it was a big risk.

In his one and only season with Ignite, Jalen helped the team to the playoffs, where they lost to the Raptors 905. Soon after, he declared himself for the NBA Draft.

Jalen was selected second overall by the Houston

Rockets in the 2021 Draft, which made him the first player ever to be drafted from the G League. He was followed soon after by players such as Jonathan Kuminga and Isaiah Todd.

He made his Summer League debut on August 8, 2021, posting 23 points, five rebounds, and two assists in a 30-minute cameo* against the Cavaliers. Jalen finished the Summer League season with All-Summer League honors but hurt his hamstring and missed the final few games.

Jalen made his NBA debut on October 20, recording nine points, four rebounds, and four assists in a 124–106 loss to the Timberwolves. Four days later, he put up 30 points, including eight three-pointers against the Celtics. The Rockets lost the game, but Jalen became the first rookie in Rockets' history to record 30 points and eight three-pointers in a single game.

Sadly, just as Jalen was hitting top form, he injured his hamstring again. He missed 14 games before returning on December 24, 2021, with 20 points in a loss to the Indiana Pacers. He had a 30-point game in an overtime win over the LA Lakers in February, then did it again the following month. He kept on recording 30-plus point games through March and April, bringing his streak to five in a row. His spectacular form led to him being named Rookie of the Month.

By the end of the season, Jalen was selected for the All-Rookie First Team, and he continued his form into the next season. In fact, he kept his 30-plus point streak going, including 34 against the Magic on November 7,

2022, which made him only the sixth guard in NBA history to score at least 30 points in 10 or more games before the age of 21!

Who are some of the others to have achieved this? Well, they include Anthony Edwards, Luka Dončić, and LaMelo Ball! It's fair to say that some truly exceptional prospects have come along over the last few years!

The records continued to fall, and Jalen recorded a career-high 42 points in a 119–114 victory over the Timberwolves on January 23, 2023, making him just the sixth player at 20 or younger to record at least three 40-point games. He didn't stop there, though, and he put up another 41 points in a game two weeks later, giving him four 40-plus games before the age of 21. Actually, he turned 21 the following day!

Jalen Green seems to be one of those players who naturally adjusts to his surroundings. No matter what team he plays against, he manages to always be one of the best players on the court. He is a natural genius with a ball, and he probably could have made it to the NBA without much effort. Yet, despite being born so talented, he still trained for five hours a day before he was even in his teens!

If he continues to practice nonstop and improve as rapidly as he has done, it's only a matter of time before he's being spoken about as a future Hall of Famer.

CADE
CUNNINGHAM

CAREER

**DETROIT
PISTONS**
2021-PRESENT

NBA DRAFT
2021
1ST ROUND
1ST OVERALL PICK

TROPHY CABINET

NBA ALL-ROOKIE FIRST TEAM	X1
CONSENSUS FIRST TEAM ALL-AMERICAN	X1
WAYMAN TISDALE AWARD	X1
NABC FRESHMAN OF THE YEAR	X1
BIG 12 PLAYER OF THE YEAR	X1

BIOGRAPHY

BORN	SEP 25, 2001
NATIONALITY	AMERICAN
BIRTHPLACE	ARLINGTON, TEXAS
HEIGHT	6 FT 6 IN (1.98 M)
POSITION(S)	PG / SG

A point guard who can score in the lane, midrange, or from the three-point line, Cade Cunningham's style is very similar to Luka Dončić. He's quick, strong, and has terrific vision on the court. At six foot six, he is devastating in the paint, and he is very hard to defend against.

Cade Cunningham was born in Arlington, Texas, on September 25, 2001. He originally wanted to play football, and he was a brilliant quarterback as a kid. He has since said that his time as a quarterback helped him with his court vision, which can be seen every time he plays today. He starred for the Texas Titans for a few years before one faithful day when he watched his brother playing basketball and decided to switch sports!

He attended Barnett Junior High School and then Bowie High School in Arlington, where he quickly became the team's best player. One of his teammates at Bowie was future pro player Kyler Edwards.

Cade averaged 15.2 points, 6.4 rebounds, and three assists in his freshman year as he helped Bowie to the District 6A Region I Final. Then, in his sophomore year, he was named District 4–6A MVP. Cade transferred to Montverde Academy for his junior year, as they had better basketball and academic programs. Montverde was ranked number one in the country by

USA Today.

While at Montverde, he teamed up with several future stars such as Greg Brown, Mike Miles Jr., Day'Ron Sharpe, and Scottie Barnes (we'll cover him next!). That Montverde team is considered one of the best rosters in the history of high school basketball.

Cade was selected for the McDonald's All-American Game at the end of his senior year, but it was canceled due to COVID-19.

Although he was considered a five-star recruit and chased by pretty much every top college in America, Cade shocked everyone when he declared for Oklahoma State. His brother, Cannen, was an assistant coach there, and Cade felt like it was the perfect place for him to flourish.

Cade was also bossing it at international level. He won gold with the United States at the 2019 FIBA Under-19 World Cup alongside Tyrese Haliburton (covered later!), Jalen Suggs, Jalen Green, and Evan Mobley (coming up later too!).

He made his college debut on November 25, 2020, recording 21 points and 10 rebounds. A few weeks later, he made the game-winning three-pointer as Oklahoma State beat Wichita State 67–64. One of his best performances came in February when he posted 40 points and 11 rebounds in a classic 94–90 overtime win.

By the end of his freshman season, Cade was recognized as a consensus First Team All-American.

He became the first Oklahoma State player to do so since 1946! As well as that fantastic achievement, he was also selected to the All-Freshman First Team and the All-Newcomer Team, as well as the All-Big 12!

Cade announced that he would enter the 2021 NBA Draft after his freshman year, and he was selected first overall by the Detroit Pistons. He injured his ankle soon after, which kept him out of preseason and the first five games of the regular season. Cade finally made his NBA debut on October 30, 2021, in a 110–103 victory over the Orlando Magic.

The Pistons fans quickly fell in love with their new rookie, especially when he recorded his first double-double in just his third game. He followed this up soon after by becoming the youngest player in NBA history to record at least 25 points, eight rebounds, and eight assists in a game. A week later, he hit a triple-double!

His averages were superb throughout his rookie season. In March 2022, he became the first rookie since the legendary Michael Jordan to average 22.9 points, seven assists, and 5.9 rebounds. Somehow, he kept these incredible averages up for the whole season yet came third in the Rookie of the Year voting. To be fair, he finished behind Scottie Barnes and Evan Mobley, so there was no real shame in coming third!

Cade's sophomore season was a disaster. After fracturing his left shin in December, he missed the rest of the season while he recovered.

Cade returned for the 2023–2024 opener on October 25, 2023, putting up 30 points and nine assists as the

Pistons lost to the Miami Heat. Three days later, he recorded 25 points and 10 assists in a 118–102 win against the Bulls. The following month, he scored a career-high 43 points against the Atlanta Hawks, but the Pistons still lost. The team was in a downward spiral, and despite Cade's great performances, the losses kept coming.

In fact, it was so bad that the Pistons created an unwanted regular season record when they lost their 27th game in a row. When they lost to the Celtics in the next game, they tied the NBA record for the most losses. Thankfully, the Pistons won two days later (an epic 129–127 win over the Raptors), which meant they didn't break the record.

Cade was immense in that victory over the Raptors, putting up 30 points and 12 assists, but his season fell apart soon after when he strained his knee in a game against the Nuggets. Much like his fractured shin the previous year, Cade missed the rest of the 2023–24 season.

Cade signed a new five-year contract on July 10, 2024, which proves how loyal he is. The Pistons might not be up to his standard just yet, but Cade clearly believes that his future lies in Detroit. If the team finds a few more rookies as good as Cade, then it won't be long until they are back in the playoffs!

SCOTTIE BARNES

CAREER

TORONTO RAPTORS
2021–PRESENT

NBA DRAFT

2021
1ST ROUND
4TH OVERALL PICK

TROPHY CABINET

NBA ALL–STAR	X1
NBA ROOKIE OF THE YEAR	X1
NBA ALL–ROOKIE FIRST TEAM	X1
THIRD–TEAM ALL–ACC	X1
ACC FRESHMAN OF THE YEAR	X1
MCDONALD'S ALL–AMERICAN	X1

BIOGRAPHY

BORN	AUG 1, 2001
NATIONALITY	AMERICAN
BIRTHPLACE	WEST PALM BEACH, FLORIDA
HEIGHT	6 FT 7 IN (2.01 M)
POSITION(S)	SF / PF / SG

You have to be special to beat Cade Cunningham and Evan Mobley in the voting for Rookie of the Year, and Scottie Barnes is just that! With a wingspan of seven foot three, Scottie is able to guard several positions at once. He might be a forward, but he can easily slot in as a guard if needed. He is a tremendous playmaker and a top-quality small forward.

Scott Wayne Barnes Jr. was born on August 1, 2001, in West Palm Beach, Florida. His father is Jamaican, and most of his family is from Canada, so Scottie grew up with lots of different influences. He attended Cardinal Newman High School in West Palm Beach, where his talents were quickly spotted. He was soon being talked about as a future NBA player despite being so young.

Scottie earned All-American honors as a freshman and never looked back. Feeling like he had learned all he could at Cardinal Newman, he transferred to NSU University School in Fort Lauderdale for his sophomore year. In his first season with NSU, he helped the team to a 36–2 record and its first-ever Class 5A state title. He was an instant hit!

He was on the move again for his senior year, transferring to Montverde Academy, which, as we know from Cade Cunningham's bio, had the number one basketball program in the country. Scottie formed a brilliant partnership with Cade on that now-famous high school team. At the end of the year, Scottie received All-American First Team honors as well as being selected for the McDonald's All-American Game, the one that was canceled due to COVID-19.

As a consensus five-star recruit, Scottie had his pick of colleges. He was also ranked as the fourth-best player in the 2020 class and the number one power forward in the country. Scottie chose Florida State, playing brilliant stuff throughout his freshman year and being named Freshman of the Year, among many other honors. That was his only college season, and he declared for the 2021 NBA Draft at the end of the year.

Scottie was selected fourth overall by the Toronto Raptors, which came as a surprise at the time as the Raptors had been expected to pick Jalen Suggs. He made his NBA debut on October 20, 2021, recording 12 points, nine rebounds, and an assist in a 98–83 loss to the Washington Wizards. Two days later, he recorded his first double-double (25 points and 13 rebounds) as the Raptors overcame the Celtics.

Scottie's great start to life in the NBA continued, and with each game, he grew in confidence. His point scoring slowly rose, and his playmaking was starting to have a positive effect on the team. He was named Eastern Conference Rookie of the Month in February 2022, which he celebrated with a then-career-high 31 points and 17 rebounds against the Lakers. Unfortunately, the Raptors ended up losing the game in overtime.

Amazingly, Scottie started all 72 games in his rookie season. His ability to excel in many different areas stood out most of all, as did his exceptional fitness. It takes a lot of energy to play every game of an NBA season, and to do it at the first time of asking is almost unheard of. To top it off, Scottie was also the only rookie in the NBA to rank in the top five in total points, rebounds, steals, blocks, and assists! He wasn't just playing every game; he was bossing them!

The Raptors reached the playoffs that year but were beaten by the 76ers in the first round. It was a close series, with Scottie doing everything he could to help the team. He was disappointed, but on an individual level, it couldn't have gone any better.

As we know, Scottie was named Rookie of the Year. The voting was close, and he was up against some phenomenal young talent. Scottie must have been proud of himself, but he is a team player, and he would surely have swapped his Rookie of the Year award for a place in the NBA Finals.

At the international level, Scottie has tasted gold three times. He was part of those amazing Under-16, Under-17, and Under-19 USA teams that won consecutive FIBA Basketball World Cups.

He has remained a star player for the Raptors since his rookie season, and his steady improvement can be seen with every passing month. He recorded his first triple-double in November 2022, and then in 2024, he appeared in the first of what is sure to be many NBA All-Star Games. He played great, recording 16 points, eight rebounds, and three assists.

Scottie's teammate Pascal Siakam was traded to the

Indiana Pacers in 2024. Before the trade, Pascal was seen as the face of the Toronto Raptors. After his departure, the Raptors promoted Scottie as the new face of the franchise. It was a lot of pressure, but Scottie has always handled that type of thing with ease.

Scottie Barnes is one of the new breed of NBA players —the type of guy who seems comfortable in almost any position on the court. Of course, he is at his most devastating as a small forward, but he could easily be one of the hottest up-and-coming guards if he wished. With his ability to control the game, he is essential to the Raptors if the team wants to challenge for the NBA title.

Beating the likes of Cade Cunningham and Evan Mobley to the Rookie of the Year award isn't easy. In fact, it takes someone of unbelievable talent to do it. Every player on this list is exceptional, and Scottie Barnes is no different in that regard. Can he reach the top? Of course he can, but he'll have to use all of that determination and talent that has got him so far already!

TYRESE
HALIBURTON

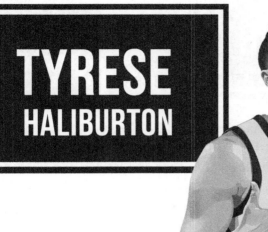

CAREER

SACRAMENTO KINGS
2020-2022
↓
INDIANA PACERS
2022-PRESENT

NBA DRAFT

2020
1ST ROUND
12TH OVERALL PICK

TROPHY CABINET

NBA ALL-STAR	X2
ALL-NBA THIRD TEAM	X1
NBA ALL-ROOKIE FIRST TEAM	X1
NBA ASSISTS LEADER	X1
SECOND-TEAM ALL-BIG 12	X1

BIOGRAPHY

BORN	FEB 29, 2000
NATIONALITY	AMERICAN
BIRTHPLACE	OSHKOSH, WISCONSIN
HEIGHT	6 FT 5 IN (1.96 M)
POSITION(S)	PG / SG

Tyrese is one of the slightly older players on this list, but he is still considered a prospect. In fact, he's one of the hottest prospects in the game. The Indiana Pacers' point guard and shooting guard has already broken the franchise's record for assists, and his three-point shooting is beyond insane. Some "team players" have been covered already, but Tyrese might just be the best of them. He has the ability to single-handedly control the game at times. A true MVP.

Born in Oshkosh, Wisconsin, on February 29, 2000, Tyrese was raised in a basketball family. His cousin Eddie Jones played in the NBA for 14 years and was a three-time All-Star. His father was a referee, and another cousin is none other than Jalen Suggs!

Tyrese was a massive WWE fan growing up, and he still loves to watch wrestling. In fact, he can often be seen in the crowd for big events such as Wrestlemania and SummerSlam! He grew up in a religious family, but Tyrese has become even more devout* as an adult. His Catholic faith is very important to him.

He attended Oshkosh High School, and as a sophomore, he was named All-Fox Valley Association (FVA) Second Team and Defensive Team. In his junior year, he was named FVA Player of the Year as the team just missed out on the state tournament title.

Tyrese really discovered his scoring form in his senior year, especially from the three-point line. In one game against Kaukauna High, he hit 42 points. Soon after, he recorded 31 points in a blistering second-half performance, shooting an incredible 18-of-18 from the free-throw line. This was in the championship game, and it gave the program its first state title.

He was considered a three-star recruit and committed to playing for Iowa State. Tyrese made his college debut on November 6, 2018, posting 12 points, four rebounds, and four assists in a 79–53 victory over Alabama State. He finished his freshman year as the only player apart from Zion Williamson to record at least 50 steals and 30 blocks.

His sophomore season was even better, in which he won Big 12 honors. He decided to forgo the rest of his college career and declared for the 2020 NBA Draft.

Tyrese was selected 12th by the Sacramento Kings and made his NBA debut on December 23, 2020, in the most dramatic way imaginable. Coming off the bench with the Kings trailing to the Nuggets, Tyrese recorded 12 points, four assists, two rebounds, and a block as the Kings won by two points in overtime.

A knee injury near the end of the season kept him out for the last seven games, but he still came third in the Rookie of the Year voting, and he was named to the NBA All-Rookie First Team.

Despite a brilliant start to the 2021–22 season, Tyrese was still traded to the Indiana Pacers alongside Buddy Hield and Tristan Thompson. Justin Holiday,

Domantas Sabonis, and Jeremy Lamb went the other way as part of the deal.

Tyrese made his Pacers debut on February 11 in a 120–113 loss to the Cleveland Cavaliers. The team might have lost, but he still recorded an impressive 23 points, six assists, three rebounds, and three steals. He posted a double-double in his second game and then repeated his double-double heroics three days later in a 113–108 victory over the Washington Wizards.

The first time Tyrese's Pacers faced his old team, the Kings, the game was a squeaker. He recorded 13 points, 15 assists, and three steals, but the Pacers lost by one point.

On April 1, Tyrese recorded 30 points in 25 minutes on 10-of-11 shooting from the field, 6-of-6 from three, and 4-of-4 from the free-throw line. It was one of the best individual performances in recent NBA memory. Sadly, the Pacers still lost the game despite Tyrese's standout performance. Two days later, he just missed out on a triple-double that included an astonishing 17 assists!

Tyrese's assists were starting to get noticed. Also, his three-pointers and brilliant shooting-to-point ratio were near-perfect. It's safe to say that the Kings already regretted trading him to the Pacers!

He began the 2022–23 season in unbelievable form, and he was named Eastern Conference Player of the Month in November as he helped the Pacers to a 3–0 start. By the end of the month, he became the first player in NBA history to record 40-plus points in a three-game streak.

He broke another record, this one a franchise record, that December when he hit 10 three-pointers in a single game. He recorded a then career-high 43 points in that game as the Pacers beat the Miami Heat. To top it off, he hit the game-winning three-pointer!

Tyrese hit another game-winning three-pointer a few months later, this time against the Bulls. The next day, he posted his 30th double-double of the season! He finished the season with his first All-Star selection and then signed a huge contract extension on July 1, 2023, on the same day it was announced that he would represent the United States at the 2023 FIBA World Cup.

One of Tyrese's proudest moments came on April 5, 2024, when he broke the Pacers' franchise record for assists when he recorded his 714th! To break such an impressive record so young takes someone very special. Tyrese kept his form up throughout the season, being named as an Eastern Conference starter for the 2024 NBA All-Star Game.

The Pacers made the playoffs, where they beat the Milwaukee Bucks in the first round. In the Semifinals, they beat the Bucks over seven games to reach the Eastern Conference Finals for the first time in a decade.

Tyrese injured his hamstring in Game 2 against the Celtics, and the Pacers crashed to a 4–0 loss in the series.

Tyrese is a phenomenal player. His ability to assist, and more importantly, his passion for setting up his teammates, makes him vital to the Pacers. He can score, and he has the composure to hit game-winning shots. That's something that can't really be coached. Calmness under pressure is something a player has deep inside, and Tyrese certainly has it. The future is certainly bright for Tyrese Haliburton and the Pacers!

EVAN MOBLEY

CAREER

CLEVELAND CAVALIERS
2021–PRESENT

NBA DRAFT

2021
1ST ROUND
3RD OVERALL PICK

TROPHY CABINET

NBA ALL–DEFENSIVE FIRST TEAM	X1
NBA ALL–ROOKIE FIRST TEAM	X1
CONSENSUS SECOND TEAM ALL–AMERICAN	X1
PAC–12 PLAYER OF THE YEAR	X1
PAC–12 DEFENSIVE PLAYER OF THE YEAR	X1

BIOGRAPHY

BORN	JUNE 18, 2001
NATIONALITY	AMERICAN
BIRTHPLACE	SAN DIEGO, CALIFORNIA
HEIGHT	6 FT 11 IN (2.11 M)
POSITION(S)	PF / C

At six foot eleven, Evan Mobley has become a rock in the Cleveland Cavaliers' defense. But that's not all his game is about. The man can score, as his records throughout his short NBA career show. He might have only been a three-star recruit out of high school, but he is certainly rated as a five-star NBA player by now!

Evan Mobley was born on June 18, 2001, in San Diego, California. His father was a former player who loved nothing more than practicing with his young kids when they were small. Evan's brother, Isaiah, who was one year older, was seen as the better player of the two growing up, and Evan didn't even like basketball that much at first!

In fact, it wasn't until the eighth grade that Evan had a growth spurt that shot him up to six foot four, and he really fell in love with the game.

Evan began playing high school basketball at Rancho Christian School in Temecula, California. He was teammates with Isaiah for three years before his brother completed his senior year. They would become teammates again in 2022 when both brothers were drafted by the Cavaliers!

Once Evan discovered organized basketball in high school, his talents rapidly improved. In his junior year, he was named California Gatorade Player of the Year and The Press-Enterprise Player of the Year. He won the Gatorade award again the following year, becoming only the second player in California basketball history to do so.

Evan was one of the young players who missed out on the McDonald's All-American Game due to COVID-19, but he was still selected, which was the most important thing. That honor opens up many doors when it comes to college recruitment!

Like Isaiah the year before, Evan was considered a five-star recruit in the 2020 class. He was also rated as one of the three best players in the country, just ahead of Cade Cunningham. He committed to playing college basketball at the University of Southern California, which was a bit of a surprise, as many of the bigger colleges were trying to recruit him.

His college debut was the stuff of dreams. He scored 21 points with nine rebounds in an overtime win against California Baptist. As a freshman, he averaged 16.4 points, 8.7 rebounds, 2.8 blocks, and 2.4 assists. He was named Pac-12 Player of the Year, Defensive Player of the Year, and Freshman Player of the Year, becoming just the second player to sweep the three awards!

Feeling like his reputation couldn't be any hotter, Evan declared himself for the 2021 NBA Draft. He was rated as the second-best prospect in the country after Cade Cunningham.

Evan was selected third overall by the Cleveland Cavaliers and made his Summer League debut against the Houston Rockets. He made his NBA debut on

October 20, putting up 17 points, nine rebounds, and six assists in a 132–121 loss to the Memphis Grizzlies. Despite missing half of that November with a sprained elbow, he was still named Rookie of the Month for games played in October and November!

On his return from injury, Evan became the first Cavaliers player since LeBron James to record five blocks in an NBA game. He played 69 games in his rookie season, starting all of them. He led rookies in blocks and rebounds, while also coming in fifth for points. It was proof that Evan wasn't just essential in defense, but he was devastating in offense too.

Evan finished second to Scottie Barnes in the Rookie of the Year voting and ahead of Cade Cunningham. It's fair to say that the 2021 NBA Draft was one of the most stacked in years!

His offensive talents were on show again on January 21, 2023, as the Cavaliers beat the Bucks 114–102. Evan recorded a career-high 38 points as he ran the show from the back, leading his team forward at every chance. It was a real breakout performance in a season full of breakout performances!

Evan then recorded 17 points, 19 rebounds, and seven blocks in a 128–105 win against the Hawks, a career-high number of rebounds and a season-high number of blocks. A month later, he underwent surgery on an injured knee that had been causing him pain for a while and missed a couple of months as the regular season came to a close.

He returned in time for the playoffs, and in Game 2 of

the Eastern Conference Semifinals, he scored a then playoff career-high 21 points and 10 rebounds in a 118–94 win over the Boston Celtics. He bettered this in Game 5, hitting 33 points, but the Cavaliers still lost the series in five games.

While Isaiah's career has taken a little longer to blossom, his younger brother, Evan, has settled into the intense challenge of playing in the NBA like it was nothing. That's the sign of a brilliant player—when they can step onto any court in the world at any time and look like one of the best players in the arena.

In addition to his fantastic few years in the NBA, Evan was also part of the United States Under-17 and Under-19 teams that won gold at the 2018 and 2019 FIBA World Cups. That generation of American players is just starting to make a name for themselves in the NBA, and future stars such as Evan and the others mentioned in this book are already becoming the faces of their respective franchises.

Evan Mobley has completely changed the Cavaliers' defense. This is proven by the fact that the team had the sixth-worst defense in the league the season before he was drafted, and the fifth-best defense in the league by the end of his rookie season. That's an unbelievable switch!

But as we've seen, Evan isn't just defensive; he can shoot just as effectively too. He's a complete player and one that everyone needs to keep an eye on in the future.

AT THE BUZZER

So, do you think it will be any easier to decide on the best prospects in basketball now that you know some of their stories? No? Yeah, it's probably even harder now that some of their amazing facts and numbers from high school and college have been revealed! It's hard to imagine being 16, like Franz Wagner, and making your professional debut against full-grown men. Or traveling to the far side of Europe and becoming the youngest player in history to sign a professional contract like LaMelo Ball.

The reason these people's stories are so exceptional is that they are exceptional people. But that's not to say that the mother who somehow manages to get her kids to school on time every day while working two jobs on the side isn't also exceptional—she is. And so is the father who shows up at every Little League game to support his kids and the teenager who goes to school every day with their head held high, even though some thoughtless kids bully them. We can all be exceptional in our own way. We just have to learn to see it.

But we're here to pick the greatest prospects in basketball, which, as you've seen, is nearly impossible!

Someone who came up a lot in the book yet didn't make the cut was Jalen Suggs. The Orlando Magic shooting guard has had a brilliant NBA career already, and he was part of those Under-16, Under-17, and Under-19 USA teams that won gold at three different World Cups. He could have easily been one of the 20 picks, but so could so many others.

Being the best at anything is hard, and basketball is no different. Of the millions and millions of hopeful kids around the world who dream of one day being an NBA legend, only a few hundred make it. There are those who won every state honor imaginable in high school, bossing it on every court they set foot on and being talked about as the next big thing, only to find out after college that they weren't all that. It's a cruel game, but that's why these elite athletes get paid so much! They're the best of the best.

All that's left is the fun part—we all get to sit back and see how these 20 stories unfold. Who will win the NBA Championship first? Who will become a Hall of Famer? Which player will lead the WNBA into a new era? Will any player on the list have their number retired? Can they continue to break records?

Who knows which of these will come true, but you can be certain of one thing—it's going to be fun finding out!

GLOSSARY

Academic - Studies, education, learning.

Cameo - A small yet important role. In sports, it's usually someone who comes onto the court or field to win the game in the last seconds, but it can just mean a short appearance.

Commonwealth Games - A smaller version of the Olympic Games, but with nations from the commonwealth, which are mainly British countries or countries ruled by Britain, but not always.

Communications - Studying communications covers things like working in social media, journalism, on TV, etc.

Deficit - The amount a team is losing by, i.e., "a 2-0 deficit."

Devout - Deep religious commitment.

Fast-tracked - Moved through or up quickly.

Founded - The place in time when a business, team, or anything was created.

Inaugural - The first of something or the start of a brand-new event, etc.

Jordan Brand Classic - An All-Star high school basketball game played every year.

K-12 - A school that teaches students from kindergarten to the 12th grade.

Meniscus - The cartilage between two joints in the body, such as the knee joint.

Minicopa Endesa - A yearly tournament between the best high school teams in Spain.

Never-say-die - A never-say-die attitude means that someone will fight until the end without ever giving up.

Nimble - Quick, light, and easy movement.

Orbital bone - The bone that protects the eyeball.

Paradise Jam - A yearly tournament that takes place on the campus of the University of the Virgin Islands.

Pro A League - The top basketball league in France.

Serie A - The top basketball league in Italy.

Understudy - Someone who learns directly from someone else, i.e., "The experienced player's understudy was a rookie."

Printed in Great Britain
by Amazon

53428258R00066